T0305095

Investing in People

THE ROYER LECTURES
1980

General Editor
JOHN M. LETICHE

Investing in People

The Economics
of Population
Quality

People

Theodore W. Schultz

UNIVERSITY OF CALIFORNIA PRESS
Berkeley · Los Angeles · London

University of California Press
Berkeley and Los Angeles, California

University of California Press, Ltd.
London, England

© 1981 by Theodore W. Schultz

First Paperback Printing 1982
ISBN 0-520-04787-7

Printed in the United States of America

1 2 3 4 5 6 7 8 9

Library of Congress Cataloging in Publication Data

Schultz, Theodore W   1902–
   Investing in people.

   (The Royer lectures ; 1980)
   Bibliography: p.
   Includes index.
   1. Human capital.   2. Education.   I. Title.
II. Title: Population quality.   III. Series: Royer
lectures ; 1980.
HD4704.7.S37   306'.3   80-6062

1 2 3 4 5 6 7 8 9

Contents

Foreword
By John M. Letiche

Written for a general as well as a professional audience, this book by the Nobel laureate Theodore W. Schultz is a fundamental contribution to the analysis of the economics of population quality, including its implications for policy throughout the world. It is path breaking in its theorizing on appropriate investment in entrepreneurial ability as a means of dealing with disequilibria pervasive in dynamic economies. The thrust of the argument, in effect, is that economic productivity and human well-being are vitally related in the poor countries as well as in the rich ones.

Professor Schultz demonstrates that a decisive factor in securing human well-being is investment in people and knowledge. He rejects the widespread but erroneous view that limitations of space, energy, cropland, and other physical properties of the earth are the decisive constraints to human betterment, and he shows that the acquired abilities of people—their education, experience, skills, and health—are basic in achieving economic progress. With illuminating brevity he explains why even the earlier giants of economics such as Adam Smith, David Ricardo, and Thomas Malthus could not have foreseen that the economic development of Western industrial nations would depend primarily on population quality. A predominant part of their national income (four-fifths in the United States) is now derived from earnings and only a small part from property. His argument, with supporting evidence, is presented in terms of the increasing value of human time; it is a brilliant formulation that I believe will become classic in economic literature.

The substance of the analysis will probably be more favorably received than his critical appraisal of policies currently practiced by donor countries and international institutions in their attempts to assist poor nations. Stressing that improvement in population quality is paramount in economic progress, Professor Schultz draws on his expertise in agriculture and development to provide fresh insights into the following fundamentals: (1) the processes whereby advances in knowledge enhance both physical and human capital; (2) the underlying reasons economists in rich countries find it exceedingly difficult to comprehend the implications of the severe resource constraints on low-income countries; (3) the nature of the preferences of poor people that determine their economic choices; and (4) the implications of the ample evidence that poor people in developing countries are no less motivated to work hard and to improve their lot, and that of their children, than are those with incomparably greater advantages.

Professor Schultz extends his analysis to show that the potential economic productivity of the poor in both developing and developed countries is not being realized because of a wide range of serious economic distortions. He devotes particular attention to the consequences of government actions upon national economies. The theory, which is clearly robust, is effectively applied to the economics of schooling in large cities, to basic research, and to economic distortions caused by the International Donor Community.

In a provocative and challenging manner, Professor Schultz demonstrates that, in the case of the United States, the federal government has a large measure of monopoly control over schooling and basic research, and that its interventions in higher education are seriously impairing the true functions of higher education. He examines the effects of the International Donor Community's injection of irrelevant equity objectives into foreign assistance programs. Further, he suggests that whereas many low-income countries have learned from their mistakes, some high-income countries—

including the United States—appear to have undergone a decline in their understanding of the fundamentals of economic productivity. Professor Schultz makes an original contribution in relating his analysis to the recent retardation in the growth of American productivity, a growth, he emphasizes, that depends on investment in entrepreneurial ability. His discussion of this issue appears to mark a breakthrough that will doubtless lead to much new theoretical-quantitative research. *

This book is based on the 1980 Royer Lectures, delivered by Professor Schultz at the University of California, Berkeley. We hope the reader will share in our gratitude for its timely preparation and our pride in its publication.

*For an elaboration of the analysis, see Theodore W. Schultz, "Investment in Entrepreneurial Ability," *Scandinavian Journal of Economics* 82 (December 1980): pp. 437-48.

Preface

There is much anxiety about food, energy, space, and other physical properties of the earth. Such anxiety is not new. It was expressed cogently at the beginning of the nineteenth century by David Ricardo and T. R. Malthus. To the extent that the present forebodings are based predominantly on assessments of the declining physical capacity of the earth, I reject them, because a valid assessment must reckon the abilities of man to deal with changes in the physical properties of the earth. These abilities are ignored in these earth-view assessments. Increases in the acquired abilities of people throughout the world and advances in useful knowledge hold the key to future economic productivity and to its contributions to human well-being.

The thrust of my argument is that the investment in population quality and in knowledge in large part determines the future prospects of mankind. When these investments are taken into account, forebodings concerning the depletion of the earth's physical resources must be rejected. A decidedly favorable achievement of many low-income countries during recent decades is their investment in population quality. Investment in research, especially in agricultural research, has also fared well. Unsolved economic issues result mainly from economic distortions of the economy by governments.

Much of my thinking and research during recent years has been devoted to the substantive issues in this book. I have published various studies on these issues, and I draw on parts of these studies with gratitude to the publishers and editors for their permission to do so. It is my pleasure to acknowledge them here: Stig Ramel, president of the Nobel Foundation; Walda Metcalf, permissions editor of the Syracuse University Press; Bikas C. Sangal, director of the International Institute for Educational Planning; R. C. O. Matthews, editor of the Proceedings of the Fifth World Congress of the International Economics Association; Walter W. McMahon and Terry G. Geske, editors of *Financing Education: Overcoming Inefficiency and Inequity* on behalf of the University of Illinois Press; Victor J. Danilov, director, Museum of Science and Industry; and V. James Rhodes, editor, *American Journal of Agricultural Economics.*

John M. Letiche persuaded me to give the Royer Lectures on which this book is based. The arrangements were ideal; I found the discussions that followed each lecture very worthwhile. Professor Letiche also made useful suggestions from which I benefited in preparing these chapters. I am grateful to James H. Clark, director, and to the editors of the University of California Press for their generous approach to my special concerns and to my style.

William K. Sellers, my secretary and administrative assistant, gave generously of his time and talents to the preparation of this book.

I am deeply indebted to Mrs. Virginia K. Thurner, my long-time editorial advisor, for her highly competent contributions.

Theodore W. Schultz
September 5, 1980

Where People Are Poor

1

The Economics of Being Poor

Most people in the world are poor. If we knew the economics of being poor, we would know much of the economics that really matters. Most of the world's poor people earn their living from agriculture. If we knew the economics of agriculture, we would know much of the economics of being poor.

Economists find it difficult to comprehend the preferences and scarcity constraints that determine the choices poor people make. We all know that most of the world's people are poor, that they earn a pittance for their labor, that half and more of their meager income is spent on food, that they reside predominantly in low-income countries, and that most of them earn their livelihood in agriculture. What many economists fail to understand is that poor people are no less concerned about improving their lot and that of their children than rich people are.

What we have learned in recent decades about the economics of agriculture will appear to most reasonably well-informed people to be paradoxical. Agriculture in many low-

This chapter is based on my Nobel lecture, December 8, 1979, Stockholm, Sweden, copyright © the Nobel Foundation 1979. I am indebted to Gary S. Becker, Milton Friedman, A. C. Harberger, D. Gale Johnson, and T. Paul Schultz for their helpful suggestions, as well as to my wife, Esther Schultz, for her insistence that what I thought was stated clearly was not clear enough.

3

income countries has the potential economic capacity to produce enough food for the still-growing population and also improve the income and welfare of poor people significantly. The decisive factors of production in improving the welfare of poor people are not space, energy, and cropland; the decisive factors are *the improvement in population quality and advances in knowledge.*

In recent decades the work of academic economists has greatly enlarged our understanding of the economics of human capital, especially the economics of research, the responses of farmers to new and profitable production techniques, the connection between production and welfare, and the economics of the family. Development economics has, however, suffered from several intellectual mistakes. The major error has been the presumption that standard economic theory is inadequate for understanding low-income countries and that a separate economic theory is needed. Models developed for this purpose were widely acclaimed, until it became evident that they were at best intellectual curiosities. Some economists reacted by turning to cultural and social explanations for the alleged poor economic performance of low-income countries, although cultural and behavioral scholars are understandably uneasy about this use of their studies. Increasing numbers of economists have now come to realize that standard economic theory is as applicable to the scarcity problems that confront low-income countries as to the corresponding problems of high-income countries.

A second mistake is the neglect of economic history. Classical economics was developed when most people in Western Europe were barely scratching out subsistence from the poor soils they tilled and were condemned to a short lifespan. As a result, early economists dealt with conditions similar to those prevailing in low-income countries today. In Ricardo's day, about half of the family income of laborers in England went for food. So it is today in many low-income countries. Marshall tells us that "English labourers' weekly wages were often less than the price of a half bushel of good wheat"[1] when Ricardo published his *Principles of Political Economy and Taxation* (1817). The weekly wage of a ploughman in India is currently somewhat less than the price of two bushels of wheat.[2] Knowledge of the experience and achievements of poor people over the ages can contribute much to an understanding of the problems and possibilities of low-income countries today. Such understanding is far more important than the most detailed and exact knowledge about the surface of the earth, or of ecology, or of tomorrow's technology.

Historical perception of population is also lacking. We extrapolate global statistics and are horrified by our interpretation of them—mainly that poor people breed like lemmings headed toward their own destruction. Yet when people were poor in our own social and economic history, that is not what happened. Expectations of destructive population growth in today's poor countries are also false.

LAND IS OVERRATED

A widely held view—the natural earth view—is that the land area suitable for growing food is virtually fixed and the supply of energy for tilling the land is being depleted. According to this view, it is impossible to continue producing enough food for the growing world population. An alternative view—the social-economic view—is that man has the ability and intelligence to lessen his dependence on cropland, traditional agriculture, and depleting sources of energy, and to reduce the real costs of producing food for the growing world population. By means of research, we discover substitutes for cropland which Ricardo could not have antic-

1. Alfred Marshall, *Principles of Economics*, 8th ed. (New York: Macmillan, 1920), p. xv.

2. Theodore W. Schultz, "On the Economics of the Increases in the Value of Human Time Over Time," in *Economic Growth and Resources*, vol. 2: *Trends and Factors*, ed. R. C. O. Matthews (London: Macmillan, 1980), the Proceedings of the Fifth World Congress of the International Economics Association, Tokyo.

ipated, and, as incomes rise, parents reveal a preference for fewer children, substituting quality for quantity of children, which Malthus could not have foreseen. Ironically, economics, long labeled the dismal science, shows that the bleak natural earth-view with respect to food is not compatible with history, which demonstrates that we can augment resources by advances in knowledge. I agree with Margaret Mead: "The future of mankind is open-ended." Mankind's future is not foreordained by space, energy, and cropland. It will be determined by the intelligent evolution of humanity.

Differences in the productivity of soils do not explain why people are poor in long-settled parts of the world. People in India have been poor for ages both on the Deccan Plateau, where the productivity of the rain-fed soils is low, and on the highly productive soils of South India. In Africa, people on the unproductive soils of the southern fringes of the Sahara, on the somewhat more productive soils on the steep slopes of the Rift landform, and on the highly productive alluvial lands along and at the mouth of the Nile all have one thing in common: they are very poor. Similarly, the much-publicized differences in land–population ratio throughout the low-income countries do not produce comparable differences in poverty. What matter most in the case of farmland are the incentives and associated opportunities farm people have to augment the effective supply of land by investments that include the contributions of agricultural research and the improvement of human skills. An integral part of the modernization of the economies of high- and low-income countries is *the decline in the economic importance of farmland and a rise in that of human capital—skills and knowledge.*

Despite economic history, economists' ideas about land are still, as a rule, those of Ricardo. But Ricardo's concept of land, "the original and indestructible powers of the soil," is no longer adequate, if ever it was. The share of national income that accrues as land rent and the associated social and political importance of landlords have declined markedly over time in high-income countries, and they are also declining in low-income countries.

Why is the Ricardian law of rent (which treats it as a result rather than a cause of prices) losing its economic sting? There are two primary reasons: first, the modernization of agriculture has over time transformed raw land into a vastly more productive resource than it was in its natural state; second, agricultural research has provided substitutes for cropland. With some local exceptions, the original soils of Europe were poor in quality. They are today highly productive. The original soils of Finland were less productive than the nearby western parts of the Soviet Union, yet today the croplands of Finland are superior. Japanese croplands were originally much inferior to those in Northern India; they are greatly superior today. In both high- and low-income countries these changes are partly the consequence of agricultural research, including the research embodied in purchased fertilizers, pesticides, insecticides, equipment, and other inputs. There are new substitutes for cropland, or land augmentation. The substitution process is well illustrated by corn: the corn acreage harvested in the United States in 1979, 33 million acres less than in 1932, produced 7.76 billion bushels, three times the amount produced in 1932.

THE QUALITY OF HUMAN AGENTS IS UNDERRATED

While land per se is not the critical factor in being poor, the human agent is: investment in improving population quality can significantly enhance the economic prospects and welfare of poor people. Child care, home and work experience, the acquisition of information and skills through schooling, and other investments in health and schooling can improve population quality. Such investments in low-income countries have been successful in improving economic prospects wherever they have not been dissipated by political instability. Poor people in low-income countries are not prisoners of an ironclad poverty equilibrium that economics is unable to break. No overwhelming forces nullify all economic improvements and cause poor people to abandon the economic struggle. It is now well documented that in agriculture poor people do respond to better opportunities.

The expectations of human agents in agriculture—farm laborers and farm entrepreneurs who both work and allocate resources—are shaped by new opportunities and by the incentives to which they respond. These incentives, explicit in the prices farmers receive for their products and in the prices they pay for producer and consumer goods and services, are greatly distorted in many low-income countries. The effect of these government-induced distortions is to reduce the economic contribution that agriculture is capable of making.

Governments tend to introduce distortions that discriminate against agriculture because internal politics generally favor urban at the expense of rural people, despite the much greater size of the rural population.[3] The political influence of urban consumers and industry enables them to exact cheap food at the expense of the vast number of rural poor. This discrimination is rationalized on the grounds that agriculture is inherently backward and that its economic contribution is of little importance despite the "Green Revolution." The lowly cultivator is presumed to be indifferent to economic incentives and strongly committed to traditional ways of cultivation. Rapid industrialization is viewed as the key to economic progress. Policy gives top priority to industry and keeps food grains cheap. It is regrettable but true that this doctrine is still supported by some donor agencies and rationalized by some economists in high-income countries.

Farmers the world over, in dealing with costs, returns, and risks, are calculating economic agents. Within their small, individual, allocative domain they are entrepreneurs tuning so subtly to economic conditions that many experts fail to recognize how efficient they are.[4] Although farmers differ in

3. For a fuller discussion, see my "On Economics and Politics of Agriculture," in *Distortions of Agricultural Incentives*, ed. Theodore W. Schultz (Bloomington, Ind.: Indiana University Press, 1978), pp. 3–23.

4. See Theodore W. Schultz, *Transforming Traditional Agriculture* (New Haven: Yale University Press, 1964; repr. New York: Arno Press, 1976).

their ability to perceive, interpret, and take appropriate action in responding to new information for reasons of schooling, health, and experience, they provide the essential human resource of entrepreneurship.[5] On most farms women are also entrepreneurs in allocating their time and using farm products and purchased goods in household production.[6] Allocative ability is supplied by millions of men and women on small-scale producing units, for agriculture is in general a highly decentralized sector of the economy. Where governments have taken over this entrepreneurial function in farming, they have been unsuccessful in providing an effective allocative substitute capable of modernizing agriculture. The allocative roles of farmers and farm women are important and their economic opportunities matter.

Entrepreneurship is also essential in research, always a venturesome business, which entails organization and allocation of scarce resources. The very essence of research is that it is a dynamic venture into the unknown or partially known. Funds, organizations, and competent scientists are necessary, but not in themselves sufficient. Research entrepreneurship is required, be it by scientists or by others engaged in the research sector of the economy. Someone must decide how to distribute the limited resources available, given the existing state of knowledge.

INEVITABILITY OF DISEQUILIBRIA

The transformation of agriculture into an increasingly productive state, a process commonly referred to as modernization, entails adjustments in farming as better oppor-

---

5. Finis Welch, "Education in Production," *Journal of Political Economy* 78 (January–February 1970): 35–59; idem, "The Role of Investments in Human Capital in Agriculture," in *Distortions of Agricultural Incentives*, pp. 259–81; Robert E. Evenson, "The Organization of Research to Improve Crops and Animals in Low-Income Countries," in *Distortions of Agricultural Incentives*, pp. 223–45.

6. Theodore W. Schultz, ed., *Economics of the Family: Marriage, Children, and Human Capital* (Chicago: University of Chicago Press, 1974).

tunities become available. The value of the ability to deal with disequilibria is high in a dynamic economy.[7] *Such disequilibria are inevitable.* They cannot be eliminated by law, by public policy, and surely not by rhetoric. Governments cannot efficiently perform the function of farm entrepreneurs.

Future historians will no doubt be puzzled by the extent to which economic incentives have been impaired during recent decades. The dominant intellectual view is antagonistic to agricultural incentives, and prevailing economic policies depreciate the function of producer incentives. D. Gale Johnson has shown that the large economic potential of agriculture in many low-income countries is not being realized.[8] Technical possibilities have become increasingly favorable, but the economic incentives that are required for farmers in these countries to realize this potential are in disarray, either because the relevant information is lacking or because the prices and costs farmers face have been distorted. For want of profitable incentives, farmers have not made the necessary investments, including the purchase of superior inputs. Intervention by government is currently the major cause of the lack of optimum economic incentives.

ACHIEVEMENTS IN POPULATION QUALITY

I now turn to measurable gains in the quality of both farm and nonfarm people. Quality in this context consists of various forms of human capital. I have argued elsewhere that while a strong case can be made for using a rigorous definition of human capital, it will be subject to the same ambiguities that continue to plague capital theory in general, and

7. See Theodore W. Schultz, "The Value of the Ability to Deal with Disequilibria," *Journal of Economic Literature* 13 (September 1975): 827–46.

8. D. Gale Johnson, "Food Production Potentials in Developing Countries: Will They Be Realized?" Bureau of Economic Studies Occasional Paper No. 1 (St. Paul, Minn.: Macalester College, 1977); idem, "International Prices and Trade in Reducing the Distortions of Incentives," in *Distortions of Agricultural Incentives*, pp. 195–215.

the concept of capital in economic growth models in particular.[9] Capital is two-faced, and what these two faces tell us about economic growth, which is a dynamic process, are, as a rule, inconsistent stories. It must be so because the cost story is a tale of sunk investments; for example, once a farmer invests in horse-drawn machinery, such machinery has little value for use with tractors. The other story pertains to the discounted value of the stream of services such capital renders, which changes with the shifting sands of growth. But worse still is the assumption, underlying capital theory and the aggregation of capital in growth models, that capital is homogeneous. Each form of capital has specific properties: a building, a tractor, a specific type of fertilizer, a tube well, and many other forms not only in agriculture but also in all other production activities. As Hicks has taught us, this capital homogeneity assumption is the disaster of capital theory.[10] It is demonstrably inappropriate in analyzing the dynamics of economic growth afloat on capital inequalities because of the differences in the rates of return, whether capital aggregation is in terms of factor costs or in terms of the discounted value of the lifetime services of its many parts. Nor would a catalogue of all existing growth models prove that these inequalities are equals.

But why try to square the circle? If we were unable to observe these inequalities, we would have to invent them, because *they are the mainspring of economic growth.* They are the mainspring because they are the compelling economic signals of growth. One of the essential parts of economic growth is thus concealed by such capital aggregation.

The value of additional human capital depends on the additional well-being that human beings derive from it. Human capital contributes to labor productivity and to entrepreneurial ability valuable in farm and nonfarm produc-

9. Theodore W. Schultz, "Human Capital: Policy Issues and Research Opportunities," in *Human Resources* (New York: National Bureau of Economic Research, 1972).

10. John Hicks, *Capital and Growth* (Oxford: Oxford University Press, 1965), chap. 3, p. 35.

tion, in household production, in the time and other resources that students allocate to their education, and in
migration to better job opportunities and better locations in
which to live. Such ability also contributes importantly to
satisfactions that are an integral part of current and future
consumption.

My approach to population quality is to treat quality as a
scarce resource, which implies that it has an economic
value and that its acquisition entails a cost. The key to analyzing the human behavior that determines the type and
amount of quality acquired over time is the relation between the returns from additional quality and the cost of
acquiring it. When the returns exceed cost, population
quality will be enhanced. This means that an increase in the
supply of any quality component is a response to a demand
for it. In this supply-demand approach to investment in population quality, all quality components are treated as durable, scarce resources useful over some period of time.

My hypothesis is that the returns on various quality components are increasing over time in many low-income countries; the returns that entrepreneurs derive from their
allocative ability rise; so do the returns on child care,
schooling, and improvements in health. Furthermore, the
rates of return are enhanced by reductions in the cost of acquiring most of these quality components. Over time, the
increased demand for quality in children, and on the part of
adults in enhancing their own quality, favors having and
rearing fewer children.[11] The movement toward quality thus
contributes to the solution of the population problem.

INVESTMENT IN HEALTH

Human-capital theory treats everyone's state of health as
a stock, i.e., as health capital, and its contribution as health

11. Gary S. Becker and Nigel Tomes, "Child Endowments and the Quantity and Quality of Children," *Journal of Political Economy* 84, pt. 2 (August
1976): S143–S162; Mark R. Rosenzweig and Kenneth I. Wolpin, "Testing the
Quantity-Quality Fertility Model: The Use of Twins as a Natural Experi-

services.[12] Part of the quality of the initial stock is inherited and part is acquired. The stock depreciates over time and at an increasing rate in later life. Gross investment in human capital entails acquisition and maintenance costs, including child care, nutrition, clothing, housing, medical services, and care of oneself. The service that health capital renders consists of "healthy time" or "sickness-free time" which contributes to work, consumption, and leisure activities.[13]

The improvements in health revealed by the longer lifespan of people in many low-income countries have undoubtedly been the most important advance in population quality. Since about 1950, life expectancy at birth has increased 40 percent or more in many of these countries. The decline in mortality among infants and very young children is only part of this achievement. The mortality of older children, youths, and adults is also down.

Ram and Schultz deal with the economics of these demographic developments in India.[14] The results correspond to those in other low-income countries. From 1951 to 1971, life expectancy at birth of males increased by 43 percent in India, and that of females by 41 percent. For both males and females, lifespans over the life cycle after age ten, twenty, and on to age sixty, were also decidedly longer in 1971 than in 1951.

The favorable economic implications of these increases in lifespan are pervasive. While the satisfactions that people derive from longer life are hard to measure, Usher has de-

---

ment," mimeographed (Yale University, Economic Growth Center, October 1978).

12. The achievements in both health and education are considered more fully in chapters 2 and 3.

13. Alan Williams, "Health Service Planning," in *Studies in Modern Economic Analysis*, ed. M. J. Artis and A. R. Nobay (Edinburgh: Blackwell, 1977), pp. 301–35; M. Grossman, *The Demand for Health*, National Bureau of Economic Research Occasional Paper No. 119 (New York: Columbia University Press, 1972).

14. Rati Ram and Theodore W. Schultz, "Life Span, Health, Savings, and Productivity," *Economic Development and Cultural Change* 27 (April 1979): 399–421.

vised an ingenious extension of economic theory to determine the utility that people derive from increases in life expectancy. His empirical analysis indicates that the additional utility increases substantially the value of personal income.[15]

Longer lifespans provide additional incentives to acquire more education, as investments in future earnings. Parents invest more in their children. More on-the-job training becomes worthwhile. The additional health capital and the other forms of human capital tend to increase the productivity of workers. Longer life results in more years of participation in the labor force, and brings about a reduction in "sick time." Better health and vitality in turn lead to more productivity per man-hour at work.

The Ram-Schultz study provides evidence of the gains in the productivity of agricultural labor in India realized as a consequence of improvements in health. Most telling is the productivity effect of the "cycle" that has characterized the malaria program.

INVESTMENT IN EDUCATION

Education accounts for much of the improvement in population quality. But in reckoning the cost of schooling, the value of the work that young children do for their parents must be included. Even for very young children during their first years of school, most parents sacrifice the value of the work that children traditionally perform.[16] Another distinc-

15. Dan Usher, "An Imputation to the Measure of Economic Growth for Changes in Life Expectancy," in *The Measurement of Economic and Social Performance*, ed. Milton Moss (New York: National Bureau of Economic Research, 1978), pp. 193–226.

16. Indra Makhija, "The Economic Contribution of Children and Its Effects on Fertility and Schooling: Rural India" (Ph.D. diss., University of Chicago, 1977); Robert L. Shortlidge, Jr., "A Social-Economic Model of School Attendance in Rural India," Cornell University Department of Agricultural Economics Occasional Paper No. 86 (Ithaca, N.Y.: Cornell University, January 1976); Mark R. Rosenzweig and Robert E. Evenson, "Fertility, Schooling and the Economic Contribution of Children in Rural India: An Econometric Analysis," *Econometrica* 45 (July 1977): 1065–79.

tive attribute of schooling is what might be called the vintage effect, as more education per child is achieved. Starting from widespread illiteracy, older people continue through life with little or no schooling, whereas the children on entering adulthood are the beneficiaries of schooling.

The population of India grew about 50 percent between 1950–51 and 1970–71. School enrollment of children aged six to fourteen rose over 200 percent, and the rate of increase in secondary schools and universities was much higher. Since schooling is primarily an investment, it is a serious error to treat all educational outlays as current consumption. This error arises from the assumption that schooling is solely a consumer good. It is misleading to treat public expenditures on schooling as "welfare" expenditures, and a use of resources that has the effect of reducing "savings." The same error occurs in the case of expenditures on health, both on public and private account.

Expenditures on schooling, including higher 'education, are a substantial fraction of national income in many low-income countries. These expenditures are large relative to the conventional national accounting measures (concepts) of savings and investment. In India, the proportional cost of schooling in relation to national income, savings, and investment is not only large, but has tended to increase substantially over time.

The Highly Skilled

In assessing population quality, it is important not to overlook the increases in the stock of physicians, other medical personnel, engineers, administrators, accountants, and various classes of research scientists and technicians.

The research capacity of a considerable number of low-income countries is impressive. There are specialized research institutes, research units within governmental departments, industrial sector research, and ongoing university research. Scientists and technicians are university trained, some of them in universities abroad. Research areas include, among others, medicine, public health (control of communicable diseases and the delivery of health services), nutrition, industry, agriculture, and even some atomic-energy research. I shall touch briefly on agricultural research, because I know it best and because it is well documented.

The founding and financing of the international agricultural research centers, originally initiated by the Rockefeller Foundation in cooperation with the government of Mexico, is an institutional innovation of a high order. But these centers, good as they are, are not a substitute for national agricultural research enterprises, as demonstrated by the increases in the number of agricultural scientists in twenty-two selected low-income countries between 1959 and 1974. All told, the number of man-years devoted to agricultural research in these countries increased more than three times during this period. By 1974, there were over 13,000 such scientists, ranging from 110 in the Ivory Coast to over 2,000 in India.[17] Indian agricultural research expenditures between 1950 and 1968 also more than tripled in real terms. An analysis by states within India shows that the rate of return has been approximately 40 percent, which is high indeed compared to the returns from most other investments to increase agricultural production.[18]

While there remains much that we do not know about the economics of being poor, our knowledge of the economic dynamics of low-income countries has advanced substantially in recent decades. We have learned that poor people are no less concerned about improving their lot and that of their children than those of us who have incomparably greater advantages. Nor are they any less competent in obtaining the maximum benefit from their limited resources. Population quality and knowledge matter. A good number of low-income countries have a positive record in improving population quality and in acquiring useful knowledge. These achievements imply favorable economic prospects,

17. James K. Boyce and Robert E. Evenson, *National and International Agricultural Research and Extension Programs* (New York: Agricultural Development Council, 1975).

18. Robert E. Evenson and Yoav Kislev, *Agricultural Research and Productivity* (New Haven: Yale University Press, 1975).

provided they are not dissipated by politics and governmental policies that discriminate against agriculture. As Alfred Marshall wrote, "Knowledge is the most powerful engine of production; it enables us to subdue Nature and satisfy our wants."

Even so, most people throughout the world continue to earn a pittance from their labor. Half, or even more, of their meager income is spent on food. Their life is harsh. Farmers in low-income countries do all they can to augment their production. What happens to these farmers is of no concern to the sun, or to the earth, or to the behavior of the monsoons and the winds that sweep the face of the earth; farmers' crops are in constant danger of being devoured by insects and pests: Nature is host to thousands of species that are hostile to the endeavors of farmers. Nature, however, can be subdued by knowledge and human abilities.

2
Investment in
Population Quality

The preceding chapter stressed the economic importance of improving the quality of the population, and the contribution of human capital to the productivity and welfare of people in low-income countries. Malthus could not have anticipated the substitution by parents of quality for quantity of children, and Ricardo could not have anticipated the development of substitutes for cropland through advances in the sciences and in agricultural research.

As a graduate student, my interest in population problems came close to being aborted. Professor Edward A. Ross was late in meeting his seminar the day his book *Standing Room Only* appeared. A Japanese student joined me at the blackboard to calculate how much of the earth's surface would be required to provide standing room for the then world's population. Our figures showed that a small part of Dane County, in which the University of Wisconsin is lo-

Both the evidence and the analysis presented here are in large part from my essay "Investment in Population Quality Throughout Low-Income Countries," in *World Population and Development: Challenges and Prospects*, ed. Philip M. Hauser (Syracuse, N.Y.: Syracuse University Press, 1979), copyright © 1979 by the United Nations Fund for Population Activities and reprinted by permission of Syracuse University Press; and from Rati Ram and Theodore W. Schultz, "Life Span, Health, Savings, and Productivity," *Economic Development and Cultural Change* 27 (April 1979): 399–421. I am indebted to Gary S. Becker, Donald McClosky, and T. Paul Schultz for their helpful comments.

cated, would suffice. Professor Ross caught us in the act. Noting his great displeasure, I opted for economics.

Modern demography is both sophisticated and rigorous in producing and handling population data. Its projections of population growth are, however, long on statistics and short on theory from the viewpoint of economics. Those for low-income countries have, in general, been exceedingly pessimistic. There has been an obsession with statistics. Computers extrapolate these with ease, and what they have been telling us is horrendous; supporting appeals to Spaceship Earth and indicating that before long the world will arrive at Ross's standing room only. But this implication is patently false. It is false with regard to the rich countries, as a look at their social and economic history when they were poor testifies. It is my contention that it is also false in the case of population growth in today's poor countries.

COUNTING THE NUMBER OF PEOPLE

Our cultural roots are mainly European, and birth and death rates were very high in Europe for many generations. The "extended" family was one of the ways of living with severe poverty; and various population explosions occurred in response to improvements in economic opportunities. Some non-European populations have, during the recent past, progressed toward a population equilibrium at a more rapid rate than European populations did. Neither Ross nor anyone else at that time anticipated the rapid decline in fertility in Japan. Viewed historically, the recent declines in the death rates and, to a lesser degree, in the birth rates of various low-income countries must be judged a remarkable social change. These declines in death and birth rates have certainly not been slow by historical standards. If they are accompanied by increases in life expectancy, as they are in many of these countries, then the economic implications are favorable. A longer life implies a real gain in welfare. The extension of the period during which people are effectively in the labor force adds to their overall productivity.

It is a major achievement that the quality of the population in many low-income countries has been rising over recent decades. Why, then, has this not been taken into account by population experts? One reason may be that it is very difficult to identify and measure quality. Population research is basically dependent on a *quantity theory of population*. Except for a small group of economists, there has been no endeavor to develop a quantity-quality theory. The basic reason is the widely held belief that rapid population growth in low-income countries forecloses the possibility of improving their population quality. This belief rests on the assumption that the resource constraints in these countries are such that they are hard pressed to increase national income and savings sufficiently to maintain the level of well-being of their rapidly growing populations and, therefore, that savings do not suffice to invest in population quality. Instead of an analysis of the social and economic processes contributing to population quality in low-income countries, the long list of issues on the research agenda related to population highlight a wide array of adverse developments. There are studies that support the belief that these countries are increasingly vulnerable to famine, to malnutrition, and to poverty. Following the food-grain production success of the Green Revolution, many analysts in India and abroad turned to making unwarranted predictions about the unfavorable side effects rather than searching for ways of duplicating the Punjabi success in other agricultural spheres.

Simple population arithmetic readily supports the belief that the creation of additional jobs to keep pace with growth in the labor force becomes increasingly less possible, so that ever more unemployment follows. Still another adverse development attributed to population growth is that it causes a decline in savings for investment as a proportion of national income. The argument is that rapid population growth implies more private consumption and more public expenditure on welfare programs, which leaves less of the national income available for savings. One of the errors in this argument is that the costs of the increases in schooling are treated as if schooling were pure consumption, whereas it is in large part an investment in an important form of human capital.

Counting the number of people measures the quantity of human beings in a population. This is what demographers do with increasing precision. Malthus developed a particular *quantity theory of population*, the dynamics of which are constrained by diminishing returns to the supporting resources. Malthus's concept of quality is a crude minimum level of quality, i.e., the subsistence of the rank and file of the population. In going beyond subsistence, the concept and measurement of population quality still consist mainly of ad hoc applications, except for recent extensions in economic theory, which is now capable of dealing with it both at the micro level (family) and at the macro level (country).

THE ECONOMIC CONCEPT OF QUALITY

The concept of quality is not new in economics. Differences in the quality of the original properties of land are an essential part of Ricardian rent. The quality of cropland, specifically its productivity, can as a rule be improved by means of investment. In general, factors of production and the goods and services that are produced differ importantly in quality.

For the purpose of this chapter, attributes of acquired population quality, which are valuable and can be augmented by appropriate investment, will be treated as human capital. Quality attributes and human abilities will be equated in order to distinguish between two basic classes of human abilities. Consider all human abilities to be either innate or acquired. Every person is born with a particular set of genes which determines his innate ability. Although there is a wide range of innate abilities, it is convenient to assume that in large populations the distributions of these innate abilities tend to be similar from one country to the next. Proceeding on this assumption, it follows that the differences in population quality between such countries are a consequence of the differences in acquired abilities.

Any element of quality that a human being acquires from

birth on entails a measure of cost. Whenever it is worthwhile to incur this cost, there is an incentive to invest in the
quality component. Child care by parents, primarily by
mothers, is a variable source of quality. So are home and
work experience, schooling, and health care. Experience derived by children from their part in family activities, and
from work in later life, is a major source of useful skills.
Economic modernization has an appreciable positive effect
in producing new opportunities and incentives to acquire
additional human capital. Learning and experimenting are
important. For example, farm people in the Punjab, in adopting the Mexican variety of wheat, experimented with a view
to obtaining needed information as they participated in the
Green Revolution. Modernization is a source of many new
experiences that entail learning valuable new skills and acquiring information of value. The positive effects of schooling are pervasive, and they will be considered in some detail,
with special reference to India, later in this chapter. Rank-
ing high in importance, too, are improvements in health.
The opportunities and incentives to invest in each of these
forms of human capital are interdependent. To understand
the actual investment in acquired human capital, it is necessary to be ever mindful of the interactions among the various processes that contribute to population quality.

The relevance of this economic approach is widely resisted by most population experts, because in their view,
economic theory is suspect when it comes to analyzing the
behavior of poor people. In the population domain, the unsettled question here is, who actually wants quality and
who is prepared to pay the price of acquiring it? Experts
often bemoan the lack of quality. Much of the population
literature implies that poor people in these countries are not
motivated to acquire human capital because they are too
strongly bound by tradition to do so. Thus, if the quality of
the population is to be improved, experts must persuade the
government to devise public programs that mandate the acquisition of quality. But this assessment of the behavior of
poor people rests on untenable assumptions. People in low-
income countries are not indifferent to opportunities that

offer worthwhile incentives to undertake investment in their own human capital. The belief that they are listless, passive creatures of habit, unperceptive of new opportunities, is not consistent with their behavior. They are, in fact, calculating human agents. Although they are poor, they tend to be efficient in allocating their meager resources with a fine regard to marginal costs and returns.

ACTIVITIES AND AN AGENDA

As already noted, the principal activities that contribute to the acquisition of human capital are child care, home and work experience, schooling, and health. The value of such added human capital depends on the additional well-being that people derive from it. It stands repeating that their well-being is enhanced by gains in labor productivity; by increases in entrepreneurial ability in acquiring information and adjusting to the disequilibria inherent in the process of modernization; by the time and other resources that students allocate to their education; by migration to better job opportunities and better locations in which to live; and, importantly, by the gains in satisfaction that are an integral part of future consumption.

The stock of acquired human capital in this context consists of abilities and information that have economic value. In ascertaining this stock at any given date, sex and age are important considerations. Both in theory and in practice, child quality is receiving increasing attention. We thus have the quality of youth and of adults,—including their activities as consumers—serving both as parents and as productive agents at work. Investment in schooling is quite manageable. It is large, given the resources available. When enhancement of this quality component is taken into account, it greatly increases the total implied savings of low-income countries.

On-the-job training and other forms of useful experience are very difficult to estimate. What can be said about the increases in such training and experience is at best based on plausible assumptions, which will be mentioned briefly when consideration is given to the implications of the improvements in health and increases in lifespan.

The achievements of many low-income countries in respect to health must be viewed as remarkable. As yet all too little is known about the precise contributions of the various public and private activities that account for the observed improvements in health. The economic implications of these achievements, however, are highly instructive and empirically testable.

HUMAN CAPITAL: FARM ENTREPRENEURS

There has been a large, measurable increase in the ability of farmers in low-income countries to modernize agricultural production. Millions of them have learned how to use land, labor, and capital efficiently in response to the production opportunities associated with agricultural modernization. They are a new breed of farmers, capable of doing what needs to be done, and no longer bound to the long-established routine of traditional agriculture.[1] Their performance in the production of more food grains is robust, despite the distortions in agricultural incentives caused by ill-advised government intervention.[2] The acquired ability of such farmers to transform the contributions of agricultural research oriented to the requirements of low-income countries and the large amounts of additional capital being committed to agricultural development and increases in food production bode well for the future, especially if the distortions in agricultural incentives are reduced.[3] With entrepreneurial talent supplied by millions of men and women on

1. The economic conditions that characterize traditional agriculture are set forth in my *Transforming Traditional Agriculture* (New Haven: Yale University Press, 1964).

2. See Theodore W. Schultz, ed., *Distortions of Agricultural Incentives* (Bloomington, Ind.: Indiana University Press, 1978).

3. D. Gale Johnson, "Food Production Potentials in Developing Countries: Will They Be Realized?" Bureau of Economic Studies Occasional Paper No. 1 (St. Paul, Minn.: Macalester College, 1977); idem, "The World Food Situation: Recent Developments and Prospects" (Chicago: University of Chicago Graduate School of Business, 1978).

small-scale producing units, agriculture is a highly decentralized sector of the economy in low-income countries.
Where governments have taken over the entrepreneurial
function in farming, they have been far from efficient in
modernizing agriculture.

One measure of the entrepreneurial ability of small farmers is the rate at which the high-yielding varieties of wheat
and rice have been adopted. New varieties adapted to the
requirements of low-income countries became available
less than two decades ago. Their suitability differed from
country to country, and new complementary inputs had to
be purchased, notably fertilizer. There were new risks, and
the appropriate changes in farm practices had to be learned.
The data in Table 1 summarize what had been achieved by
1976–77.

The ability of farmers in low-income countries to perceive, interpret, and respond to new events in a context of
risk is an important part of the human capital of these countries. In economics, this particular ability is treated as the
entrepreneurial ability of farmers. The observed increase in
this ability is one of the components contributing to the
quality of the population.

Although I have featured farmers, increases in the ability
to reallocate resources in response to new events is not restricted to farm entrepreneurs.[4] People who supply labor services for hire or who are self-employed are also reallocating
their services in response to changes in the value of the
work they do. So are housewives in using purchased goods
and services in household production. Students, likewise,
are reallocating their own time along with the educational
services they purchase as they respond to changes in expected earnings and in the personal satisfactions they expect
to derive from their education. Consumption opportunities
are also changing and, inasmuch as pure consumption entails time, here, too, people are reallocating their own time
in response to changing opportunities. Clearly, in an econ-

4. An extended analysis of this ability appears in my article "Investment
in Entrepreneurial Ability," *Scandinavian Journal of Economics* 82 (December 1980).

Table 1 CROP LAND DEVOTED TO HIGH-YIELDING VARIETIES
OF WHEAT AND RICE, 1976–77

	High-Yielding Varieties Planted (in millions of hectares)[a]		High-Yielding Varieties as a Percentage of Total Individual Crop Area	
	Wheat	Rice	Wheat	Rice
South and East Asia	19.7	24.2	74.2	30.4
Near East (West Asia and North Africa)	4.4	.04	17.0	3.4
Africa (excluding North Africa) ..	.2	.12	22.5	1.7
Latin America[b] ...	5.1	.92	41.0	13.0
Total	29.4	25.28	44.2	27.5

SOURCE: Data from Dana G. Dalrymple, *Development and Spread of High Yielding Varieties of Wheat and Rice in the Less Developed Nations*, USDA Foreign Agricultural Economic Report No. 95 (1978), pp. x–xi.
[a] Either planted or harvested area.
[b] A rough estimate.

omy that is undergoing modernization, the value of the ability to reallocate resources in response to new events is pervasive. Although it is, as a rule, more difficult to identify and measure the increase in the allocative ability of nonfarm people than of farmers, judging from the studies that have been made it is plausible that this entrepreneurial ability has been increasing throughout the populations of many low-income countries. *The supply curve of entrepreneurial ability has been shifting to the right.*[5]

INVESTMENT IN CHILD QUALITY

The arithmetic of the increasing numbers of children in low-income countries seems fairly simple compared to the

5. See my "The Value of the Ability to Deal with Disequilibria," *Journal of Economic Literature* 13 (September 1975): 827–46. To show this supply

task of determining whether or not the quality per child has risen over time. The care provided by parents, public health programs, and early schooling are investments in child quality. Have these improved in the low-income countries? Are infants and children of tender ages receiving a better start in life than they did two or three decades ago? Although infant mortality has declined markedly, there is no reliable direct evidence. The measurement of these attributes of child quality throughout the population in any low-income country is at best exceedingly difficult. Some insights pertaining to child care can, however, be inferred from the implications of theory, along with some indirect evidence in support of these implications.

The response of households to new products and child care facilities that are more efficient relative to their costs than the traditional ones is, in principle, similar to the response of farmers to new high-yielding wheat and rice varieties and public irrigation facilities. Many households in low-income countries have been purchasing new antibiotics and acquiring advice and information from new health centers. Members of these households benefit from various public school and health programs. Studies that feature malnutrition are not designed to measure the changes in the nutrition of populations by country over time. Food consumption per capita has in general been increasing, albeit

---

curve graphically, scale the economic value of entrepreneurs' ability vertically and the quantity horizontally. The economic value is the *rent* they derive from their allocative ability. The rent for any given ability is a function of the disequilibria that entrepreneurs face. The amount of entrepreneurial ability is a function of the original ability of human agents, their experience in dealing with disequilibria, their schooling, and their health. For traditional agriculture, which has long been in a state of equilibrium, production activities tend to be routine, and there is little or no rent from entrepreneurial ability. This supply curve is far to the left in the graph, indicating a small amount of revealed entrepreneurial ability, because it has little value under such equilibrium conditions. Once agricultural modernization is under way, the rent derived from allocative ability becomes important, and the entrepreneurial ability of farmers is increased by learning from experience, by the acquisition of more schooling, and by improvements in health. The supply curve therefore appears definitely to the right of that indicated for traditional agriculture.

slowly. The implication is that nutrition has been improving.

In analyzing the behavior of households, there is a private demand for useful drugs, for schooling, for health services, and for more and higher quality food. The supply curve of these products and services has been shifting to the right, and they are available at a lower price than in the past. Housewives in general perceive, interpret, and (when they find the new opportunities worthwhile) respond to the implied incentives to improve the welfare of the family, including the well-being of their children. There is also a public demand for programs to improve the supply of drinking water and reduce the incidence of waterborne disease.

The indirect evidence that supports the hypothesis that child quality has been increasing in low-income countries takes three forms. Per capita food consumption has increased somewhat. Preprimary and primary school enrollment has been rising substantially relative to the number of children. And, most telling, there is an increase in the survival rate of children. The figures in Table 2 are obtained by dividing the number of living children by the total number born to women of specific ages. The survival rates of the children of women aged thirty to thirty-four are compared with those of mothers aged fifty to fifty-four. For each of the eleven countries, the survival rate of the children of younger women is clearly better than for those of older women. In eight of these countries, it is in the neighborhood of 20 percent higher. It is noteworthy that the rural survival rates are somewhat lower than the urban ones in all but one of the countries for which estimates by residence are shown.

There are a considerable number of economic studies that pertain to child quality, but in using the relevant theory, most of the empirical work deals with family behavior in high-income countries. Leibowitz's analysis of investment in children shows that home investments increase the measured stock of childhood human capital.[6] Even within a sample of very able children, the home investment variables

6. Arleen Leibowitz, "Home Investment in Children," in *Economics of the Family: Marriage, Children, and Human Capital,* ed. Theodore W. Schultz (Chicago: University of Chicago Press, 1974).

Table 2 SURVIVAL RATE OF CHILDREN BY AGE OF WOMEN AND BY RESIDENCE, WHERE AVAILABLE[a]

	Children of young mothers (age 30–34)	Children of older mothers	Relative increase in survival rates for young mothers in percent
Taiwan, 1967			
Five Cities	.963	.772 age 60+	20
Other Area	.930	.753 age 60+	19
Malaysia, 1970—			
Sarawak			
Urban	.961	.933 age 50+	3
Rural	.894	.807 age 50+	10
Korea (South), 1970			
Cities	.945	.709 age 60+	25
Countryside . . .	.925	.702 age 60+	24
Liberia, 1970			
Urban	.88	.77 age 50+	12
Rural	.84	.72 age 50+	14
Brazil			
1940	.782	.683 age 50+	13
1970	.870	.780 age 50+	10
Syria, 1970			
Urban	.859	.642 age 50+	25
Rural	.805	.595 age 50+	26
Tanzania, 1967			
Urban	.84	.67 age 50+	20
Rural	.74	.58 age 50+	22
El Salvador, 1971			
Urban	.837	.664 age 50+	21
Rural	.816	.666 age 50+	18
Indonesia, 1965 . .	.779	.634 age 50+	19
Jordan, 1961			
Urban	.777	.576 ages 55–59	26
Rural	.731	.570 ages 55–59	22
Central African Republic (year not indicated)	.67	.51 age 50+	24

SOURCE: T. Paul Schultz, "Interrelationship Between Morality and Fertility," in *Population and Development*, ed. Ronald G. Ridker (Baltimore: Johns Hopkins University Press, 1976).
[a] The survival rate is the average number of living children divided by the average number of children ever born.

were positively and significantly related to her measure of the children's human capital. The positive effect of the allocation of time by parents to their preschool children on their education is also reported by Hill and Stafford.[7] With the advantage of the contributions of various earlier studies, De Tray analyzes child schooling in a recent RAND study.[8]

The approach of Butz and Habicht to the effects of nutrition and health rests on the assumption that family response behavior to new and better opportunities is in principle similar to that of farmers in low-income countries.[9]

The interaction in family behavior between child quantity and quality of children is high on the research agenda of human-capital oriented economists. De Tray's Ph.D. research deals directly with substitution between quantity and quality of children in the household.[10] His analysis was then extended, concentrating on child quality and the demand for children. His tentative findings, using U.S. data, are that the mother's education increases the relative efficiency with which child quality is produced.[11] In a seminal theoretical paper, Becker and Lewis then expanded the analytical framework of the interaction between quantity and quality of children.[12] They concluded that "the observed price elasticity of quantity exceeds that of quality, just the opposite of our conclusion for observed income elasticities. This reversal of quantity-quality ordering for price and income elasticities . . . gives a consistent interpretation of the

7. Russell C. Hill and Frank P. Stafford, "The Allocation of Time to Preschool Children and Educational Opportunity," *Journal of Human Resources* 9 (Summer 1974): 323–41.

8. Dennis N. De Tray, *Child Schooling and Family Size* (Santa Monica, Calif.: RAND Corp., April 1978).

9. William P. Butz and Jean-Pierre Habicht, "The Effects of Nutrition and Health on Fertility," in *Population and Development*, ed. Ronald G. Ridker (Baltimore: Johns Hopkins University Press, 1976).

10. Dennis N. De Tray, "The Substitution Between Quantity and Quality of Children in the Household" (Ph.D. diss., University of Chicago, 1972).

11. Dennis N. De Tray, "Child Quality and the Demand for Children," in *Economics of the Family*, ed. Schultz.

12. Gary S. Becker and H. Gregg Lewis, "Interaction Between Quantity and Quality of Children," in *Economics of the Family*, ed. Schultz.

findings of De Tray and others." In extending the Becker-Lewis model, some additional determinants of the demand for the quality of children are presented by Becker.[13] Further progress in analyzing this set of interactions is reported by Becker and Tomes.[14] A unique test of the quantity-quality model by Rosenzweig and Wolpin, using the twins experiment in a national sample of 2,939 farm households in India, shows the theoretically expected negative effects of twins on schooling.[15]

SCHOOLING: AN INVESTMENT IN QUALITY

Schooling is more than a consumption activity, in the sense that it is not undertaken solely to obtain satisfactions or utility while attending school. On the contrary, the public and private costs of schooling are incurred deliberately to acquire a productive stock, embodied in human beings, that provides future services. These services consist of future earnings, future ability in self-employment and household activity, and future consumer satisfactions. As an investment, schooling adds appreciably to the savings of low-income countries, but it is omitted in the conventional national economic accounts because the reported savings are confined to the formation of physical capital.

There are a considerable number of studies that show that the supply of entrepreneurial ability is definitely increased by additional schooling. My survey of these studies clearly shows the pervasiveness of the favorable effects of schooling on the ability to deal with disequilibria associated with economic modernization.[16] The studies pertaining to agricul-

13. Gary S. Becker, "A Theory of Social Interaction," *Journal of Political Economy* 82 (November–December 1974): 1063–93.

14. Gary S. Becker and Nigel Tomes, "Child Endowments and the Quantity and Quality of Children," *Journal of Political Economy* 84, pt. 2 (August 1976): S143–S162.

15. Mark R. Rosenzweig and Kenneth I. Wolpin, "Testing the Quantity-Quality Fertility Model: The Use of Twins as a Natural Experiment," mimeographed (Yale University, Economic Growth Center, October 1978).

16. Schultz, "The Value of the Ability to Deal with Disequilibria," cited above.

Table 3 POPULATION AND EDUCATIONAL ENROLLMENT
INCREASES, INDIA, 1950–51 TO 1970–71

	1950–51	1970–71	1973–74	Percentage increase from 1950–51 to 1970–71
Population (millions)				
Total	361	548	580	52
Age 6–10 ...	44.5	75.2	NA	69
Age 11–14 ..	32.0	51.0	NA	59
Enrollment (millions)				
Primary	18.7	59.3	63.2	217
Middle	3.3 ⎫4.8	13.4 ⎫20.6	14.7	306 ⎫329
Secondary ...	1.5 ⎭	7.2 ⎭	7.5	980 ⎭
Post-secondary ...	2.0	5.2	NA	160
University ..	.17	1.95	2.23	1047

SOURCE: Population estimates for 1950–51 and 1970–71 are from the 1951 and 1971 census of India and for 1973–74 from Reports on Population and Family Planning, Population Council, New York. Enrollment estimates are from Government of India Planning Commission, *Draft Five Year Plan, 1978–83* (1978), p. 226, except for postsecondary estimates from Rati Ram and Theodore W. Schultz, "Life Span, Health, Savings, and Productivity," *Economic Development and Cultural Change* 27 (April 1979): 399–421.

ture provide the best evidence on this issue, mainly because the data are better than they are for other types of economic activity. Welch's recent essay is a further contribution, extending the analysis of the role of human capital in agriculture.[17]

The value of the contribution of the work that very young

17. Finis Welch, "The Role of Investments in Human Capital in Agriculture," in *Distortions of Agricultural Incentives*, ed. Theodore W. Schultz (Bloomington: Indiana University Press, 1978).

Table 4 INVESTMENT IN SCHOOLING RELATIVE TO NATIONAL
INCOME, INDIA, 1950–51 TO 1970–71

	1950–51	1970–71
1. National income in billion rupees, current prices	95.1	344
2. Public schooling expenditures in billion rupees, current prices	1.1	10.8
3. Private opportunity cost of students' time in billion rupees, current prices	3.9	27.9
4. 2 + 3 as a percentage of 1	5	11

SOURCE: Rati Ram and Theodore W. Schultz, "Life Span, Health, Savings,
and Productivity," *Economic Development and Cultural Change* 27 (April
1979): 399–421.

children do at home and on family farms in India, and the
effects that this cost component has upon school attendance, is a major part of the Ph.D. research by Makhija.[18]
She also surveys the literature bearing on this issue, including the recent studies by Shortlidge and by Rosenzweig and
Evenson.[19]

The increase in schooling relative to population growth in
India is indicated by Ram and Schultz. As Table 3 shows,
over the period from 1950–51 to 1970–71, the population increased by 52 percent, while preprimary and primary enrollment rose by 217 percent and middle and secondary school
enrollment by 329 percent.

The remarkable increase in public school expenditures
and in private opportunity cost of students relative to the
increase in national income in India is evident in Table 4.

18. Indra Makhija, "The Economic Contribution of Children and Its
Effects on Fertility and Schooling: Rural India" (Ph.D. diss., University of
Chicago, 1977).

19. Robert L. Shortlidge, Jr., "A Social-Economic Model of School Attendance in Rural India," Cornell University Department of Agricultural Economics Occasional Paper No. 86 (Ithaca, New York: Cornell University, Jan-

As noted in chapter 1, schooling is primarily an investment in future earnings and future satisfactions, and it is a serious error to treat educational outlays as current consumption. This error arises from the assumption that schooling is a consumer good like food, and from the treatment of the increases in public expenditures on schooling associated with population growth as "welfare" expenditures, a burden on the state, and a use of resources that has the effect of reducing "savings" that would otherwise be available for investment purposes. In India, as Table 4 shows, the proportion that schooling expenditures bear to national income, savings, and investment is not only large, but has tended to increase substantially over time.

THE STOCK OF HEALTH

A house built to last fifty years adds a good deal more to the stock of housing than does a house that lasts only thirty years. Quality of construction makes the difference and the better house is the more valuable property. Human capital has comparable dimensions. The economic value of human capital, be it entrepreneurship, skills, or schooling, is enhanced when its useful life is extended. The life expectancy of a population is an important factor both in determining the incentives to invest in various forms of human capital and the value of the stock of such capital.[20] Despite the emphasis that has been put on the adverse effects it has in causing population growth, there is no other quality attribute that is as important and pervasive as improved health in its contributions to the welfare of people in low-income countries. It is obvious that the large decline in death rates and persistently high traditional birth rates (which, however, are now beginning to fall substantially) account for most pre-

uary 1976); Mark R. Rosenzweig and Robert E. Evenson, "Fertility, Schooling and the Economic Contribution of Children in Rural India," *Econometrica* 45 (July 1977): 1065–79.

20. This section draws primarily on the study of Rati Ram and Theodore W. Schultz, "Life Span, Health, Savings, and Productivity," *Economic Development and Cultural Change* 27 (April 1979): 399–421.

vailing population growth. But what has been overlooked is that population growth is not necessarily incompatible with advances in human welfare. On the contrary, there are important favorable consequences of increases in lifespan. Usher has developed means of determining the additional utility that people derive from increases in life expectancy. His application of this extension of theory to particular low-income countries suggests that the real rate of economic growth is appreciably higher than shown by the national statistics of these countries.[21]

There is also a set of implications that pertain to the incentives to acquire more human capital, namely the incentive to acquire more schooling and on-the-job experience as investments in future earnings and the incentive on the part of parents to invest more in the human capital of their children. Gains in the state of health and longer lifespan also imply increases in the productivity of workers as a consequence of longer participation in the labor force, greater physical ability to do work, and less loss of working time because of illness.

Since about 1950, life expectancy at birth has increased 40 percent or more in many low-income countries. This remarkable achievement has, however, received all too little attention. The people of Western Europe and North America never attained so large an increase in life expectancy in so short a period. Since there are no comparable developments in Western economic history to account for this unprecedented achievement on the part of many low-income countries, to analyze its effects calls for a direct appeal to the human condition and circumstances that have characterized these countries.

The gains in life expectancy achieved by low-income countries are well illustrated by developments in India. Over the period from 1951 to 1971, life expectancy at birth of males rose from 32.4 to 46.4 years, and that of females from

21. Dan Usher, "An Imputation to the Measure of Economic Growth for Changes in Life Expectancy," in *The Measurement of Economic and Social Performance*, ed. Milton Moss (New York: National Bureau of Economic Research, 1978), pp. 193–226.

Table 5 INCREASE IN LIFE EXPECTANCY OF MALES AND FEMALES IN INDIA BETWEEN 1951 AND 1971 AT SELECTED AGES

Age	Life Expectancy				Increase 1951–1971			
	Males		Females		Males		Females	
	1951	1971	1951	1971	Years	Percentage	Years	Percentage
10	39.0	48.8	39.5	47.7	9.8	25	8.2	21
20	33.0	41.1	32.9	39.9	8.1	25	7.0	21
30	26.6	33.3	26.2	32.0	6.7	25	5.8	22
40	20.5	25.9	21.1	25.4	5.4	26	4.3	20
50	14.9	19.2	16.2	19.7	4.3	29	3.5	22
60	10.1	13.6	11.3	13.8	3.5	35	2.5	22

SOURCES: 1951—Census of India 1951, Paper No. 2 of 1956, pp. 35–38; 1971—Census of India 1971, Paper No. 1 of 1977, pp. 16–19. Rati Ram and Theodore W. Schultz, "Life Span, Health, Savings, and Productivity," Economic Development and Cultural Change 27 (April 1979): 399–421.

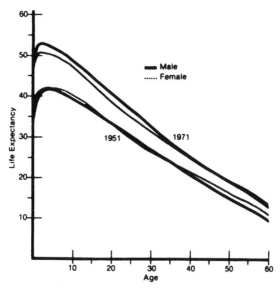

Figure 1. Age-Specific Life Expectancy, India, 1951 and 1971 Censuses

SOURCE: Rati Ram and Theodore W. Schultz, "Life Span, Health, Savings, and Productivity," *Economic Development and Cultural Change* 27 (April 1979).

31.7 to 44.7 years. The notable increases in life expectancy that occurred over these two decades are shown for selected ages from ten to sixty in Table 5. The full range from birth to age sixty of these increases in life expectancy is depicted in Figure 1; the difference in years in favor of 1971 is shown on the vertical scale.

The Ram-Schultz study provides some evidence on the gains in the productivity of agricultural labor in India that have been realized as a consequence of improvements in health. Using a simple production-function approach to account for the increases in agricultural production during each of two recent decades, the unexplained part of the increases in output is approximately 36 percent from 1951 to 1961 and only 19 percent from 1961 to 1971. These unexplained residuals in this growth-accounting approach are attributed to "technical progress" and to the consequence of the improvement in the health of workers. The difference between the magnitudes of these two residuals (36 and 19 percent respectively) presents a puzzle. The Green Revolution, the hallmark of technical progress, was actively under-way during the later decade. It was not so during the 1951–61 period. Yet this residual was larger during the decade before the Green Revolution occurred. In searching for a solution to this puzzle, we found that the differences in the production effects of improvements in the health of the labor force appear to be the explanation. Public health programs initiated during the first five-year plan (1951–56) and carried on through the second plan (1956–61) had a much larger favorable effect on health than did the programs undertaken later. The program to suppress malaria tells the story. Official data indicate that the incidence of malaria dropped from 75 million cases in 1952–53 to about 1.1 million in 1959–60. But the malaria program suffered a setback after 1965, although the incidence of malaria did not revert to the old level.

The observable difference in the decline in mortality alone explains about 28 percent of the interstate variation in agricultural productivity. An additional test, based on the effects of the suppression of malaria by districts in India, shows that crop output in "high incidence" districts rose 45 percent, while in "low incidence" districts the increase was less, as expected, namely 38.6 percent. The evidence seems reasonably good in support of the proposition that the near-eradication of malaria during the early part of the decades under consideration contributed significantly to increases in agricultural production. What applies to the favorable production effects of malaria programs also applies to the other public and private activities that lead to improvements in health and increases in life expectancy.[22]

Human-capital theory is sufficiently robust to gauge particular improvements in population quality. Many low-

22. Other studies on the favorable productive effects of malaria control lending support to this analysis are Robin Barlow, "The Economic Effects of Malaria Eradication," *American Economic Review* 57, pt. 2 (May 1967): 130–48; Jere Behrman, *Supply Response in Underdeveloped Agriculture: A Case Study of Four Major Annual Crops in Thailand, 1937–63* (Amsterdam: North Holland Publishing Co., 1967); G. Borkar, *Health in Independent India* (New Delhi: Ministry of Health, Government of India, 1957);

income countries have during the past two or three decades made large investments in the various stocks of capital that are embodied in people. The growth in the stock of health capital is most impressive. The improvement in health that accounts for the 40 percent and more increase in life expectancy is an unprecedented achievement, in which people of all ages have participated. Child quality has risen. When account is taken of the large increases in schooling per pupil and the gains in health, the quality of school-age children and young adults is clearly much better than it was for the equivalent age-classes some decades ago. The effects of additional schooling and improvements in health on labor productivity have been favorable. Entrepreneurship has increased considerably throughout the economy; people are taking more effective advantage of the new economic opportunities associated with modernization. Annual savings have also been enhanced substantially by the investment in human capital.

In a society where life is short, labor earns a pittance; work is hard and life is harsh. Vitality is low, illiteracy abounds, and people languish. A turn to a better future comes when the span of life increases. Incentives become worthwhile. Invest in more schooling, and the time spent at work becomes more productive. Investment in human capital and the resulting improvements in population quality matter. "Standing room only" becomes a myth.

Wilfred Malenbaum, "Health and Productivity in Poor Areas," in *Empirical Studies in Health Economics*, ed. H. E. Klarman (Baltimore: Johns Hopkins University Press, 1970); Rati Ram, "India's Agriculture During 1950–70: An Exercise in Growth Source Analysis," University of Chicago Agricultural Economics Paper No. 74–14 (1974); N. V. Sovani, *Population Trends and Agriculture Development: Case Studies of Sri Lanka and India*, United Nations Economic and Social Council Paper E/Conf. 60/SYM 1/11 (April 1973); C. E. A. Winslow, *The Cost of Sickness and the Price of Health* (Geneva: World Health Organization, 1951); and *Health: Sector Working Paper* (Washington, D.C.: World Bank, 1975).

Achievements in
Higher Education

Higher education the world over is being severely criticized. It has become fashionable to assail the performance of colleges and universities. There is hostility to universities because of their commitment to the advancement of the sciences, to the technology that the sciences spawn, and to economics. Many critics contend that colleges and universities are unconcerned about social and economic reforms, are not supporting government policies wholeheartedly, and disregard equity in admission of students and appointment of faculty.

Low-income countries are not spared. The International Donor Community is wary of supporting higher education in such countries. (Aid for agricultural research and, to some extent, to institutions training health personnel are exceptions.) Moreover, host governments do not like having donor agencies intervene in higher education.

In view of all that is deemed to be wrong in higher education, is there any point in appealing to economic analysis? No doubt an economist should be wary of entering upon this hazardous terrain. Yet, even where data are inadequate,

A substantial part of this chapter is based on my essay "The Value of Education in Low Income Countries: An Economist's View," to be published in *Higher Education and the New International Order* by the International Institute for Educational Planning (IIEP/UNESCO, Paris). I am indebted to C. Arnold Anderson, Mary Jean Bowman, and Charles M. Hardin for their helpful comments.

in many low-income countries economic theory has much relevance. The plausibility of the implications of theory can be considered and, in some cases, they can be tested empirically. Higher education in any society is a specialized, costly activity. Scarce resources are allocated to support colleges and universities, and the services they render are valuable. The costs of higher education can be reckoned more readily than can its value.

A good deal can, however, be inferred from the costs that is important in understanding the allocation of resources to higher education. For example, over a decade ago Panchamukhi showed that for India the total costs of university and professional education over the decade 1950–51 to 1959–60 came to about 700 crores of rupees.[1] Over three-fifths of these costs were private, mainly earnings foregone by the students. The inference is clear that, in analyzing the relevant allocative behavior, it is essential to consider both private and public allocations. Whereas the private allocations to higher education of parents and students are often ignored, they in fact exceed public expenditures.

I digress here to mention a problem that is very much in the foreground in considering the results of investment in education: What is it about economic growth that reduces the difference in relative earnings between workers who have little and those who have much education? We know that this difference has declined appreciably in the United States over recent decades. For the purpose at hand, a study by Kothari comparing these differences in earnings in Bombay and in the United States is instructive.[2] He found that in the city of Bombay in 1955 and 1956 the mean income of people classified as "higher professionals" was virtually eight times as much as that of unskilled laborers, whereas in the United States in 1959 it was only three to one. The

1. P. R. Panchamukhi, "Educational Capital in India," *Indian Economic Journal* 12 (January–March 1965): 306–14; Table 1, p. 309. For a more comprehensive study, see V. N. Kothari, "Factor Cost of Education in India," *Indian Economic Journal* 13 (April–June 1966): 631–46.

2. V. N. Kothari, "Disparities in Relative Earnings Among Different Countries," *Economic Journal* 80 (September 1970): 605–16.

puzzle is resolved by analyzing the absolute differences; whether or not a college education is worthwhile, it is the absolute gains in earnings and not the relative difference that determine whether the costs of a higher education and the expected higher earnings make it a worthwhile investment.

My purpose is to understand the actual private behavior of people and the behavior of their governments as it is revealed in their allocation of resources in acquiring the services rendered by colleges and universities. The information that is needed for this purpose is in short supply. We know that parents, students, and public agencies make their allocative decisions on the basis of information that is far from perfect. Every investment in higher education, regardless of the form it takes, is a forward, long-run, future commitment, and is therefore beset with risk and uncertainty. Under these circumstances, individual families and governments must learn from experience. It is fair to say that many governmental agencies have learned that manpower planning does not provide a solution for the allocation problem related to higher education. No economic planning model can solve this problem. No computer can print the instructions that will tell public bodies or students what investments they should make in higher education. The limitations of formal educational planning models have been competently set forth in various studies during recent years. I find the review of these studies by Psacharopoulos useful and to the point.[3] It covers what has been done in educational planning in the last twenty years, and traces the evolution of key theories and methodologies, including the present state of the art.

Development in low-income countries involves several important factors that play a relatively small role in development in high-income countries. Before I examine these

3. George Psacharopoulos, "Educational Planning: Past and Present," *Prospects* 8, no. 2 (1978). There are three other perceptive papers that should be mentioned here: Mark Blaug, "Educational Policy and the Economics of Education: Some Practical Lessons for Educational Planners in Developing Countries," and Michel Debeauvais, "The Contribution of the

factors there are three related considerations that call for a brief comment: the scarcity of capital, the long-term nature of most investments in higher education, and the longer lag in public than in private behavior in learning from experience.

It is of course obvious that low-income countries do not have the luxury of abundant capital. As their development proceeds, the demand for additional capital increases markedly. Whatever the form of investment, an ever-present constraint is the availability of funds. Even where the rate of savings is high, the amount is small, because income per capita is low compared to that in high-income countries. In chapters 1 and 2, I emphasized the fact that national economic accounts understate actual savings by a wide margin because both public and private expenditures on schooling and in higher education are omitted from the investment accounts.

Capital from foreign sources for higher education is understandably suspect. Whether such capital comes from foreign governments, from the World Bank, from other United Nations sources, or from private foundations, the terms on which it is available are viewed by the receiving country as likely to have some adverse influence on what the host government deems to be the purposes of its colleges and universities. Although foreign capital to construct a steel mill or an irrigation facility is not free of outside influence, countries find it more manageable than in the case of higher education.

Additions to the stock of educational capital as a rule render services for many years. A college or university education serves most students over most of their lives. Expenditures on buildings and facilities for education are long-term investments, and the annual budget to support the faculty is also, in principle, a long-term commitment, even though se-

Economics of Education to Aid Policies: A Critical Comment," both in *Education and Development Reconsidered*, ed. F. Champion Ward (New York: Praeger, 1974); and Mary Jean Bowman and C. Arnold Anderson, "Theoretical Considerations in Educational Planning," in *Educational Planning*, ed. Don Adams (Syracuse, N.Y.: Syracuse University Press, 1965).

curity of tenure of individuals is frequently violated. The building up of a corps of well-qualified agricultural scientists who are also members of a university faculty—one of the major achievements of a number of low-income countries—is clearly a long-term enterprise. Most research has a long-term dimension, and research that contributes to the modernization of agriculture usually takes years to be consummated.[4]

In economic affairs, contrary to widely held belief, public bodies are slower than individuals in perceiving, interpreting, and responding appropriately to changes in economic conditions. This difference in adjustment lags is clearly evident in agriculture, for example, in the promptness of farmers in adopting the more profitable high-yielding crop varieties compared to the slowness of governments in altering their price policies in line with changes in the value of wheat relative to that of rice. Millions of farmers throughout the low-income countries have demonstrated that they are alert to better opportunities, and act promptly to take advantage of these by reallocating the resources in their small domain. Governments are slow in learning that policies must be adjusted as economic conditions change. It is remarkable how well farmers have performed despite the distortions in agricultural incentives from ill-advised interventions by governments.[5] Similar disparities between public and private lags characterize other economic sectors, as well as higher education. As unanticipated events and developments occur, parents and students respond more promptly than public bodies do.

THE DYNAMICS OF DEVELOPMENT

Development constantly rearranges all manner of economic options, and economic disequilibria abound. Living

4. Theodore W. Schultz, "The Economics of Research and Agricultural Productivity," International Agricultural Development Service Occasional Paper (New York, 1979).

5. Theodore W. Schultz, ed., *Distortions of Agricultural Incentives*, (Bloomington, Ind.: Indiana University Press, 1978).

with and adjusting to the dynamics of development is akin to the baffling experiences of teenagers during their years of rapid growth. Firms, households, sectors, and regions within a country get out of balance with each other, and so does higher education. Economic disequilibria are inherent in the process of modernization.[6]

The economic processes of development are much the same in low- and high-income countries. The stock of capital must be augmented by means of investment in both physical and human capital, and by adjusting to changes in the relative prices of products and production factors, including changes in the value of the services rendered by human agents. These adjustments entail reallocating the available resources as economic conditions change. As activities, these are all means to the end of maximizing the satisfactions and thereby the welfare of the people served by the economy.

The relevant data are better for India than for most other low-income countries, and there are useful studies of the politics and the economics of higher education to draw upon.[7] Compared to most other countries in this class, India has measurably democratized her colleges and universities without incurring serious instability. Among the larger countries, the higher-education record of Brazil and Mexico is in some major respects similar, but useful data are harder to come by.

Although there has been considerable governmental intervention, higher education in India has not been critically politicized, as has happened in many countries, with resulting instability and disorganization which have greatly impaired university instruction and research. (Argentina is a notable example.) The higher-education policy of China during recent decades can usefully be compared to the policy of

6. See my "On Economics and Politics of Agriculture," in *Distortions of Agricultural Incentives*.

7. Susanne Hoeber Rudolph and Lloyd I. Rudolph, *Education and Politics in India* (Cambridge, Mass.: Harvard University Press, 1972). I find the approach and analysis of the studies in this book excellent and also very useful.

India throughout the period since her independence. Higher education has provided India with many trained young professionals in the various sciences, in engineering, in medicine, and in agricultural research.[8] China now acknowledges that as a consequence of the disorganization of higher education during recent decades, she faces a serious shortage in young professionals.

During the past three decades, a small corps of economists has concentrated its analytical work on human capital. Economic theory has been extended to make room for human capital as an integral part of capital theory. Increasing attention is being given to the allocation of the time of individuals, to the value of the time of women in household production and in the labor force, to marriage and fertility, and more generally to the economics of the family.

The process of development in many low-income countries is benefiting appreciably from indigenous university-trained professionals in engineering, technology, medicine, public and private administrative work, and agriculture. The high-yielding Mexican wheat had, for example, several genetic limitations under Indian conditions. In a few years Indian agricultural scientists modified and improved the genetic composition of the Mexican wheat appreciably, and in doing so reduced these limitations. This achievement on the part of Indian scientists was possible because India already had a sizable stock of this specialized scientific ability. Universities in India had contributed substantially to the training of her scientists in these skills.

The Economic Importance of Human Skills

Natural resources, physical capital, and raw labor are not sufficient in developing a highly productive economy. A wide array of human skills are essential in fueling the dynamics of development. Without them, the economic prospects are bleak. Many experts overrate the necessity of hav-

8. From 1960–61 through 1963–64 the universities of India accepted 185 doctoral theses in agriculture. Doctoral theses accepted in engineering/technology, commerce, and medicine were 78, 69, and 57 respectively. See Rudolph and Rudolph, cited above, p. 42.

ing natural resources on national territory. The economic successes of the early Mediterranean city-states, of the free cities of northern Europe, and, currently, of Hong Kong and Singapore, do not support this need. Nor do the economic successes that Denmark, Switzerland, and Japan have achieved.

Historical perspective on literacy in early modernization, and on the role of education in economic development during recent decades, is provided by Anderson and Bowman,[9] who trace the linkage between early industrialization in the West and literacy, and argue that literacy was more important than has usually been acknowledged. They show that the development and transmission of practical knowledge and intellectual skills are at the heart of economic development, observing in conclusion that:

> . . . a dynamic economy can be launched and sustained only through the efforts of men at all social levels who embody both conventional learning and technical-manipulative skills—including specifically skills in the decoding of instructions and the "debugging" of new processes. A complex economy rests on widely diffused tools for communication, storage, and retrieval of knowledge.

It is easy to overlook the strong private demand for higher education in many low-income countries. It is difficult for most observers from an affluent country to explain the inordinate growth in private demand for such education. Governments do not compel students to attend colleges and universities; on the contrary, despite the increasing number of higher-education institutions, the demand for admissions exceeds the supply of places by a wide margin. The cited study by Rudolph and Rudolph leaves little room for doubt that in India admissions have been very much rationed since independence. Even for one who is aware of the proliferation of colleges and universities in the United States, it is diffi-

9. C. Arnold Anderson and Mary Jean Bowman, "Education and Economic Modernization in Historical Perspective," in *Schooling and Society: Studies in the History of Education*, ed. Lawrence Stone (Baltimore: Johns Hopkins University Press, 1976), pp. 3–19.

cult to comprehend what has been occurring in India. In 1950–51, India already had 695 colleges and 28 universities; as of 1973–74 there were 4,308 colleges and 104 universities.[10] The implied increase in the private demand for higher education is extraordinary. Parents have been making enormous sacrifices in order to provide higher education for their children. But we forget that this was so before the turn of the century for many parents in the United States.

Higher Education and Research

Many critics of higher education in low-income countries err in undervaluing the contributions of research to economic growth. It is wishful thinking to argue that if there must be research, let the rich countries indulge in this form of "conspicuous consumption." Expenditures on research and development are, of course, large in high-income countries. But what is too often overlooked, even by those who see the value of research, is that low-income countries must also acquire a substantial research capacity. They must be able not only to take advantage of the advances in research elsewhere but also to serve the unique requirements of their own economies. Fortunately, despite the critics, the research achievement of a considerable number of low-income countries is impressive. The list of research activities is long and expenditures for research are not small given the resources of these countries.

Indian expenditures on agricultural research between 1950 and 1968, for example, rose from 52 to 177 million rupees, in constant 1968 prices, and this expenditure as a percent of the value of agricultural production increased from .07 to .17 percent.[11] Evenson and Kislev have traced the agricultural production effects by states within India and they estimate the rate of return on this investment in research to be 40 percent.[12]

10. Government of India Planning Commission, *Draft Five Year Plan, 1978–83* (1978), Appendix 1, p. 226.
11. Robert E. Evenson and Yoav Kislev, *Agricultural Research and Productivity* (New Haven, Conn.: Yale University Press, 1975), Table 6.2.
12. Ibid., Table 6.3 and p. 101.

Table 6 gives the flavor of the size and the remarkable increases in the number of agricultural scientists between 1959 and 1974 in twenty-two selected low-income countries. A comment is called for on the numbers of publications shown in the last column. Annual publications reporting agricultural research results by country are by no means the best measure of performance. Rate-of-return studies of the type that Evenson and Kislev did for India are vastly better, but until more such studies are at hand, publication counts provide some useful information.

EXPECTATIONS VERSUS POSSIBILITIES

Higher education is seemingly not meeting the expectations of the proponents of a new international order. It is said that higher education in low-income countries is not relevant to the social "needs" of these countries, and that it increases social inequality by creating elitism. Higher education is even blamed for the rural exodus. Unemployment of college and university graduates is another part of the indictment. Critics conclude that higher education and organized university research in low-income countries have become obsolete.

The opposition between this perspective and my position arises primarily out of a difference in what is expected of higher education. Endeavors to implement expectations that exceed what is possible result in distortions in the allocation of resources. Recognition of the limits of what is possible is therefore necessary in any analysis of expectations, equally applicable to the production of firms, households, or industries. Wherever products or services are produced, the production possibilities are always limited by the available resources, by the ability of human agents, and by the organization of production activities. For instance, although the production possibilities of farms in the Punjab have increased greatly during the last two decades, they are nevertheless much below those of Iowa farms in the United States. Higher education is also always limited by the availability of resources, the quality of the faculty and the orga-

Table 6 AGRICULTURAL RESEARCH EXPENDITURES, SCIENTIST MAN-YEARS, AND SCIENTIFIC PUBLICATIONS
FOR SELECTED LOW-INCOME COUNTRIES, 1959 AND 1974

	Expenditures[a]		Scientist Man-Years		Average Annual Publications
	1959 (× 1,000)	1974 (× 1,000)	1959	1974	1969–73
Argentina	$12,000	$ 24,000	320	880	85
Brazil	4,800	48,800	200	2,000	130
Chile	720	4,390	32	192	26
Colombia	6,000	13,300	200	870	36
Mexico	2,160	9,760	190	1,000	39
UAR	4,800	8,950	400	800	165
Ghana	1,440	2,440	60	140	25
Ivory Coast ...	2,400	5,130	40	110	12
Nigeria	6,010	16,270	110	300	63
Senegal	1,560	3,250	45	160	4
Kenya	610	3,660	25	280	30
Iran	1,800	14,640	170	500	34
Turkey	2,040	9,760	55	580	23
Sri Lanka	1,320	2,440	50	130	18

India	10,570	26,030	1,150	2,150	1,278
Pakistan	960	2,030	120	280	90
Indonesia	240	3,420	15	380	13
Malaysia	1,440	4,880	40	240	27
Philippines	1,800	5,210	200	620	70
Thailand	660	4,880	150	725	18
South Korea ..	1,080	2,440	300	650	37
Taiwan	840	2,360	250	400	60
TOTALS	$65,250	$218,040	4,122	13,387	2,283

SOURCE: James K. Boyce and Robert E. Evenson, *Agricultural Research and Extension Programs* (New York: Agricultural Development Council, 1975), Table 2.1 and Appendix II.
ᵃIn constant 1971 U.S. dollars.

nization and administration of colleges and universities. These limitations are not a consequence of esoteric factors. In fact, the production possibilities of higher education are severely limited in systematic and measurable respects.

Expectations of higher education, however, appear to be virtually unlimited, when one considers the statements of many critics. This does not apply to faculties and students nor to the administrators of colleges and universities. Although the expectations of governments are often less constrained by the realities of the relevant production possibilities, even they are, in general, far less extreme than the expectations of many experts.

The approach that gives rise to the problem of the extraordinarily large gap between expectations and possibilities is propelled by ideas that are strongly committed to the perfectibility of man and of society. Its normative objective is an ideal society, a utopian world in which people would not be selfish, and competition for scarce resources would not be required.

By comparison, the alternative advocated here postulates a society and a policy that encompass the infirmities of human nature, the selfish and ambitious behavior of people, and the struggle to acquire, hold, and use scarce resources. The normative objective of this approach differs significantly from that of the utopian ideal. An important part of the difference is that the second approach relies on actual, observable behavior, and its implications are for that reason testable. It is not restricted to economics. It is also essential in analyzing political behavior.

In economics, for the purpose at hand, this approach is unglamorous, matter-of-fact, and mundane. It is a behavioral analysis to determine the observable demand for, and supply of, higher education under various conditions. The supply is constrained by the production possibilities of colleges and universities; and the demand is constrained by the costs of acquiring the services of higher education and by the income of parents, students, and governments. That it is useful in analyzing the politics of education is evident from the work of Rudolph and Rudolph:

We do not assume . . . that there is such a thing as an educational system free of political intervention; nor do we assume that such a thing would be good. In a democratic society and in educational institutions that receive government funds, there will be political influence . . . The real questions focus on distinguishing what type of political pressure and politicization is benign and what is not . . . whether education purposes are subsumed by the political system, or whether politics becomes a means for strengthening or redefining educational goals.[13]

The two approaches presented above differ greatly with respect to expectations pertaining to education.[14] Much confusion and controversy arises from the failure to distinguish between them.

I am keenly aware that the demand-and-supply analysis of an economist applied to higher education is anathema to some professional educators, to many governments, and above all to those critics who are strongly committed to the first approach to higher education. One proceeds at one's own peril in discussing the substance of these expectations and their feasibility. The conventional hedge is to camouflage one's own values and wear the mantle of academic innocence. Let me proceed unprotected!

On the normative grounds peculiar to advocates of certain types of utopias, higher education should eschew the sciences and their technological offspring. Since the achievements of a number of low-income countries have, as I have shown, in no small part been made possible by advances in the sciences and associated technology, I find this particular utopia untenable.

13. Rudolph and Rudolph, *Education and Politics in India*, p. 95. Despite its title, this analysis at many points deals with the scarcity of resources as well as the value of education, and exhibits a fine appreciation of the underlying economics.

14. See Charles M. Hardin, "Conflicting Views on the World Food Problem—A Socialist or Capitalist Orientation: Which is Preferable?" (University of California, Davis, November 1978). This paper is precisely the kind of scholarly analysis and criticism that is all too rare in the area of higher education. Professor Hardin has to his credit several studies pertaining to the influence of politics on land-grant colleges and universities in the United States.

A pervasive normative expectation of the devotees of certain ideal societies is, moreover, that higher education should support wholeheartedly, without reservation and with no criticism, the government of its home country—be it communism, socialism, or liberal democracy; a centrally controlled or a capitalistic economy. This expectation is, however, rarely evoked evenhandedly. More often than not, it is expected that criticism by academic scholars is warranted in capitalistic countries, but that it should be off limits in other countries. For the government of any country to take a jaundiced view of criticism of its internal affairs by foreign scholars is understandable. But woe unto the country that forecloses the criticism of its own scholars. All governments make mistakes. Internal scholarly criticism is essential in identifying such mistakes, in analyzing their origins and consequences, and in indicating the changes required to correct them. To propose that there be no scholarly criticism in this area of human affairs is counterproductive.

Social reforms have become the order of the day. In high-income countries, where subsistence of the poorer people is no longer a pressing issue, there is widespread public commitment to reduce inequality in the distribution of personal income. Most countries sooner or later learn that it is more difficult than had been anticipated to make large income transfers without seriously impairing the efficiency of the economy. Modified or alternative reforms to achieve the same purpose are being called for and devised. But the equity-efficiency[15] issue is far from settled in either rich or poor countries, although the options available differ greatly between them. Discrimination prevails by sex, color, language, religion, ethnicity, and citizenship versus noncitizenship. Other reforms seek to reduce pollution, to increase the safety of work places, and to improve health. The issue here pertains to the expectation that higher education should

15. See Theodore W. Schultz, ed., *Investment in Education: The Equity-Efficiency Quandary*, a supplement to the *Journal of Political Economy* 80, pt. 2 (May–June 1972).

produce reformers and that colleges and universities should become active reform agents. But experience in the United States and elsewhere has shown that however "liberalizing" college may seem to be, students are not transformed into reformers by mere instruction. Students' ideas of a good society and their commitment to reforms are rooted in their personal values, which are only marginally influenced by education. The normative expectation that higher education can inculcate new values that eliminate the self-interest of students greatly exceeds the ability of colleges and universities to do so, even if this were desirable.

Should the purpose of scientific and applied technical research be to achieve advances in the sciences and in technology that will solve the problem of inequality in the personal distribution of income? My comment on this particular normative expectation is restricted to agricultural research. In this area, for example, it is impossible for plant breeders to produce superior varieties of wheat and rice that will grow only on small farms. The equity problem pertaining to small versus large farms, like the income distribution problem in general, is a political problem in the fundamental sense that meaningful solutions depend on public policies and programs. Science cannot solve this problem.

The founding and the size of colleges and universities, their internal organization and administration, are important issues. So are the management interventions of governments.[16] The allocation of public funds to educational institutions inevitably calls for accountability in the uses that are made of these funds. With regard to political interventions, it is essential to distinguish between accountability— including interventions to strengthen and redefine educational goals—and the politicization of higher education that distorts the real functions of higher education. Nor is the

16. The history of their establishment by the U.S. government and the slow, gradual development of the land-grant colleges and universities is exceedingly instructive on these issues. See Mary Jean Bowman, "The Land-Grant Colleges and Universities in Human Resource Development," *Journal of Economic History* 22, no. 8 (December 1962): 523–46.

intervention of some private interests and local public bodies always benign. To treat these issues adequately would call for another major essay. Fortunately, they have been examined competently and carefully in the case of India by Rudolph and Rudolph.[17]

Higher education is essential in the orderly developments of low-income countries. Although the function of higher education is seriously impaired by governments in many countries, the achievements in higher education in an increasing number of them are substantial.

17. In *Education and Politics in India,* cited above.

As the Value of
Human Time Increases

4
The Economics of the Value of Human Time

The difference in the economic value of human time between low- and high-income countries is very large. At the time when the foundations of classical economics were established, however, the value of human time throughout Western Europe was exceedingly low. In view of economic changes since then, are corresponding improvements possible for low-income countries? While it is all too convenient to believe that it can be accomplished by law supported by rhetoric, it is clearly not possible to achieve this objective on command by government. Increases in the earnings of labor depend basically on achieving increases in the value productivity of labor. Investment in population quality is one of the important means of doing so. The economic dynamics are, however, exceedingly complex, as is evident in accounting for the increases in the value of human time that have occurred over time in high-income countries.

In the United States, for instance, real earnings per hour of work have risen fivefold since 1900. The economic dynamics that account for this remarkable increase in the value of human time are as yet only dimly understood. There are a number of instructive puzzles, however, that provide clues.

The overarching economic puzzle is that the vast increase in the stock of capital which has taken place in high-income countries has not, in general, resulted in observable diminishing returns. Why this has not occurred is at the heart of

Knight's inquiry into the unsettled issue of diminishing returns to investment.[1] The decline in the economic importance of Ricardian rent as a fraction of national income has
also received all too little attention. Closely related is the
remarkable decline of the agricultural sector relative to the
rest of the economy in its contribution to national income.
Then, too, there is the relative decline of the manufacturing
sector in high-income countries. In international trade theory there is the implication that countries with relatively
large stocks of capital have a comparative advantage in exporting capital goods and importing products that are labor
intensive. But, in fact, countries with relatively large stocks
of capital have acquired a comparative advantage in exporting various classes of goods that are highly labor intensive
(the Leontief paradox).[2] Corresponding changes have been
occurring within the economies of major high-income
countries. Puzzles abound with respect to the changes over
time in the earnings of labor, among them the marked decline in the income derived from property relative to that
from earnings. The rate of return on investment in human
capital has tended to exceed the rate of return on investment
in physical capital. The central issue is the increase in the
economic value of human time.[3]

As noted in chapter 1, in Ricardo's day "English labourers'
weekly wages were often less than the price of half a bushel
of good wheat."[4] The weekly wage of unskilled workers in
the United States was at that time equivalent to two bushels
of wheat, and in 1890, when Marshall's *Principles* appeared,

1. Frank H. Knight, "Diminishing Returns From Investment," *Journal of
Political Economy* 52 (March 1944): 26–47.

2. W. Leontief, "Introduction to a Theory of the Internal Structure of
Functional Relationships," *Econometrica* 15 (October 1947): 361–73.

3. This unsettled issue has long been on my research agenda, and I have
considered it in a number of papers. My most extensive analysis appears in
Economic Growth and Resources, vol. 2: *Trends and Factors*, ed. R. C. O.
Matthews (London: Macmillan, 1980), pp. 107–29. The Proceedings of the
Fifth World Congress of the International Economic Association, Tokyo.
The remainder of this chapter draws in large part on that essay.

4. Alfred Marshall, *Principles of Economics*, 8th ed. (New York: Macmillan, 1920), p. xv.

had increased close to nine bushels. By 1970 the weekly compensation of manufacturing production workers was sufficient to buy 96 bushels of high quality wheat.[5] The economics of the decline in the deflated price of wheat by half between 1900 and 1970 is well known. But the economics of the rise in real wages for time spent at work by labor, which is vastly more important, is still in large part unsettled. This rise in the value of human time is, in large part, a consequence of the formation of new kinds of human capital in response to economic incentives. The most important achievement of modern economic growth is undoubtedly this increase in the stock of human capital.

The concept of human capital treats earnings foregone as a part of the cost of its acquisition, and leads to the theory of the allocation of time, to the household production function, and to models for analyzing the price and income effects of the value of the time of women in household activities, including the bearing and rearing of children. These advances have made possible a wide array of empirical studies. Of the factors that determine the price of human time, a good deal is now known about those that determine the supply, but knowledge about the demand is still fragmentary. Measurement of real changes in the value of time has received all too little attention.

MEASUREMENT

Measures of the price of wheat come easily. The market specifications of hard red winter wheat are well established; Kansas City is the major market; and the price per bushel is readily available. But the attributes of the services of labor differ widely by occupation in any year, and they change over time. For the many people in the labor market, compensation for time spent at work presently falls into two

5. See Appendix: Table A. It may be said that the 1970 price of wheat was unrealistically low in view of the events in the early seventies. It is true that wheat prices soared, but they then declined sharply as production increased. By August 1977, a week's wages was equal to the price of 110 bushels of wheat.

parts: money paid as wages and various wage supplements.‸ In the United States prior to 1936, wage supplements were less than one cent per hour. By 1957 these supplements had risen to sixteen cents, and by the seventies they added an estimated 13 *percent* to wages paid.

Actual time spent at work is a significant variable. Official statistics of hourly earnings overstate the time spent at work because they do not adjust for increases in paid vacations, holidays, and sick leave. Nor do they exclude time devoted to lunch periods, coffee breaks, wash-up time, call-in time, and jury duty.[7]

Estimates of changes in actual real hourly wages are not precise when one uses the Consumer Price Index. Consumer prices have various limitations for the purpose at hand. But even if the CPI were a perfect measure of the purchasing power of dollar wages, it is incorrect to apply this index to wage supplements invested in pensions and other future benefits, the real value of which depends on the price level when these future benefits are received. As Rees has noted, there is presently no satisfactory solution of this problem.[8] Obviously the same difficulty arises in adjusting the wages paid to workers by this index to the extent that their wages are added to savings.

We shall use Rees's estimates because they account for most of the more important wage supplements and get fairly close to the actual time spent at work. We have brought his estimates up to date, and have adjusted his estimates and our own to 1967 dollars, using the official CPI, mindful as we do this of the unsolved problems this adjustment entails. Clearly the composition of the labor force does not remain constant in terms of age and sex distribution; health has become better, lifespan has increased, young people spend more years in school and are thus older when they enter the

6. See Albert Rees, "Pattern of Wages, Prices and Productivity," in *Wages, Prices, Profits, and Productivity*, the Proceedings of the American Assembly (New York: Columbia University Press, June 1959), pp. 11–35, for the components that account for these wage supplements and Rees's estimates of them from 1929 to 1957, which appear in his Table 1, p. 15.

. 7. Ibid.   8. Ibid., p. 13.

labor market, and the aged can afford to retire earlier than formerly. The years of education of workers have been increasing at a high rate. The attributes of those working for wages or salaries since 1900 differ substantially from decade to decade.

We can use either of two approaches in dealing with the problem of the changing attributes of the labor force in estimating the price paid for an hour of a worker's time. We could construct a labor price index, comparable to the Consumer Price Index, which would indicate the changes in the level of wages and salaries over time. Or we can assume that there is a pattern of normal wages and that this may change from one subperiod to the next. This approach rests on the assumption that the wages of the various major subsets of workers stay approximately the same relative to one another during the subperiod. The advantage is that the array of such wages may be treated, for the purpose of functional, allocative economics, as if there were a normal wage.

We shall treat the total hourly compensation of production workers in manufacturing for actual time spent at work as the *normal wage*. Manufacturing workers are the largest part of the labor force. Retail trade workers are the second largest group, and although their numbers have been increasing rapidly relative to manufacturing workers, the level of their hourly wages has stayed at about 70 percent of that of manufacturing workers.[9] As will become evident presently, the real earnings of educated people, when due allowance is made for the cost of their education, are determined in the long run by normal wages, that is, by what the labor market pays for the services of the rank and file of labor. This means that over any long period, the real earnings, for example, of elementary and secondary school teachers, of academic faculties, and of other college-educated people are the sum of normal wages and of the additional compensation that is required to have made their education worthwhile. It may be easier to see the dependency on nor-

9. See the *Economic Report of the President*, (Washington, D.C.: Council of Economic Advisers, 1976), Tables B–27 and B–28.

mal wages in the case of real wages in agriculture. They, too, are determined primarily by the rise in normal wages throughout the economy and not by particular agricultural events.

In our attempt at measurement, we are mainly concerned with the price of human time—that is, the price that is paid for an hour of that time. It is well to be explicit on this point. Economic growth theories tend to omit the changes that occur over time in the relative prices of the services of the factors of production. Since the relative price of human time has been increasing greatly, the omission of this change in relative prices means that there is no reckoning of such price effects on incentives in allocating currently available resources and in investing to enhance the future stock of capital. Price effects matter; the resulting income effects follow.

In the United States, hourly compensation for time spent at work for the part of the labor force to which we turn for our normal wages increased in 1967 dollars from about $.60 to $3.27 between 1900 and 1970, or well over fivefold (see Table 7). When we partition this long upward trend into four subperiods, each beginning and ending when the economy was performing well, the annual rates for each are as follows:[10]

Subperiod	Annual Rate
1900–15	1.4
1915–30	2.4
1930–50	3.7
1950–70	2.12

We now turn (Table 8) to the hourly earnings of unskilled workers, teachers, and associate professors. It should be

10. Another way of describing these changes is to note that real hourly wages rose slowly from 1900 to the middle of the next decade, sharply during World War I, and slowly throughout the twenties and early thirties. There then followed a strong upward trend for two and a half decades, after which wages rose less strongly once again from the late fifties to 1970. The years which show a decline are 1904, 1907, and 1908, and then 1914, 1919, 1921, 1922, 1925, 1932, 1945, and 1946.

Table 7 COMPENSATION OF MANUFACTURING PRODUCTION
WORKERS IN THE UNITED STATES, 1900–1975

Year	Consumer Prices (1967 = 100)	Hourly Wages (1967 Dollars)	Hourly Wage Index (1900 = 100)
1900	25	$ .60	100
1910	29	.70	117
1920	60	.92	153
1930	50	1.06	177
1940	42	1.60	267
1950	72	2.15	358
1960	89	2.85	475
1970	116	3.27	545
1972	125	3.44	573
1975	161	3.37	562

SOURCE: Hourly wages are Albert Rees's estimates of total compensation
per hour of work of manufacturing production workers in *Long Term
Economic Growth, 1860–1970* (Washington, D.C.: U.S. Bureau of Economic Analysis, 1973), Appendix 2, B70, pp. 222–23. They are updated
and adjusted from 1957 to 1967 dollars.

borne in mind that wage supplements are not included for
the unskilled. An adjustment for such supplements is included in the hourly earnings of teachers and associate
professors.[11]

The change in the absolute differences holds the key to
whether or not it is worthwhile to invest in human capital,
mainly in education, for the purpose of increasing (future)
earnings. Manufacturing workers in 1900 received only $.02
more per hour (in 1967 dollars) than the unskilled; teachers,
$.24 more; and associate professors, $2.02 more. By 1970
these absolute differences were $.79, $1.91, and $3.70 re-

11. The academic market for associate professors is more active than
that for professors; it is therefore subject to shorter lags in adjusting to
changes in normal wages and in the costs of acquiring the required professional skills than is the case for those who have attained the rank of
professor.

Table 8 COMPARISON OF EARNINGS BY CATEGORY, 1900 AND 1970

	Hourly Earnings in 1900[a]	Hourly Earnings in 1970[a]	Relative Percentage Increase (1900 = 100)	Absolute Increase, 1900 over 1970[a]
Manufacturing workers	.60	3.27	545	2.67
Unskilled workers	.58	2.48	427	1.90
Teachers	.82	4.39	535	3.57
Associate professors	2.60	6.18	238	3.58

SOURCE: Appendix: Table B.
[a]In 1967 dollars.

spectively. The difference in favor of associate professors is the largest, although it increased much less relatively than the other three groups over this long period.

The first two subperiods in this seventy-year period cover fifteen years each; the second two cover twenty years each. The U.S. labor force increased by 37 percent from 1900 to 1915, by 26 percent during the next fifteen years, and by 35 percent during each of the subsequent subperiods. The unemployment rate was 5 percent in 1900 and 4.9 in 1970. In 1950 it was 5.3 percent. On this score, 1913 would have been a better date than 1915, and 1929 better than 1930, because the unemployment rate was 4.3 in 1913 and 3.2 in 1929. Table 9 gives the increases in real hourly earnings for each of these four subperiods.

In analyzing the allocation of resources as of any given year when stocks of such resources are given, employees and employers respond to the relative prices of the productive services of these resources. The prices for work time during each of the five dates encompassing our four subperiods, shown in Table 10, indicate that our measure of normal wages (those of manufacturing workers) rose gradually by about a third over the 1900 to 1970 period relative to un-

Table 9 PERCENTAGE INCREASE IN EARNINGS, 1900–1970

	1915 over 1900	1930 over 1915	1950 over 1930	1970 over 1950
Manufacturing workers	23	43	103	52
Unskilled workers ...	21	37	72	50
Teachers	32	38	54	91
Associate professors	20	8	7	72

SOURCE: Appendix: Table B.

skilled wages. Recall, however, that no wage supplements are here reckoned in for the unskilled. The hourly salary of teachers tended to be about 50 percent above that of the unskilled for each of these dates. But the relative price of the time of associate professors declined markedly.

To the best of my knowledge, there are no complete time-series estimates of hourly earnings for other countries where earnings are high that are comparable to those presented for the United States. Phelps Brown's indexes of real annual wages in industry (see Table 11) are, however, useful in this connection.[12] The upward trends in real wages in industry in France, Germany, Sweden, and the United Kingdom shown in Table 11 are much like that in the United States, with some notable differences. France and the United Kingdom show no increase between 1900 and 1910, and, as of 1925, the increases show Sweden and the United States substantially ahead of the other three countries (was this a

12. In interpreting the increases in real wages shown in Table 11, it should be borne in mind that we are now dealing with real annual wages in industry, not hourly wages. They are less complete in getting at the total compensation of employees than the estimates by Rees. Accordingly, Rees's estimates show a higher rate of increase than Brown's. Thus, for the United States during the period from 1900 to 1970, Brown's real wages show a fourfold increase and Rees's real hourly compensation a strong fivefold rise.

Table 10 RELATIVE REAL HOURLY EARNINGS
(UNSKILLED = 100)

	1900	1915	1930	1950	1970
Unskilled workers	100	100	100	100	100
Manufacturing workers* ...	103	106	110	130	132
Teachers	141	154	155	139	155
Associate professors	448	444	350	218	249

SOURCE: Appendix: Table B.
*From Albert Rees, "Pattern of Wages, Prices and Productivity," in Wages, Prices, Profits, and Productivity, Proceedings of the American Assembly (New York: Columbia University Press, June 1959).

consequence mainly of differences in the effects of the war and its aftermath?). Sweden and the United States maintain their advantage over the others up to 1960, with the United Kingdom losing ground in relative terms. Finally, at the end of the sixties, France and Germany join Sweden and the United States in showing a fourfold and more relative increase in real annual wages in industry over the period from 1900 to 1970, whereas the relative increase for the United Kingdom is slightly less than threefold.

This attempt at measurement supports five observations pertaining to increases in the value of human time: (1) in the United States the interaction between the preference to engage in work for pay and the availability of opportunities has resulted in a very large increase in the real hourly compensation for time spent at work; (2) while the evidence presented is fragmentary, it is consistent with the findings of recent human-capital studies in showing that the relative difference between the real hourly earnings of wage workers and of highly educated workers in the labor market has become smaller over time; (3) the absolute difference between these two classes of workers has become larger, however, presumably sufficiently so to have provided compensation for the rising cost of the additional education and to have induced relatively more people to acquire such education; (4) the secular rise in the real earnings of labor in industry in the four selected European countries suggests a process sim-

Table 11 INDEXES OF REAL WAGES IN INDUSTRY IN FRANCE,
GERMANY, SWEDEN, THE UNITED KINGDOM, AND THE UNITED
STATES, 1900–1970. (1890–1899 = 100)

	France	Germany	Sweden	United Kingdom	United States
1900	112	108	110	104	110
1910	112	116	131	104	121
1925	135	127	158	113	160
1930	138	156	183	124	160
1938	142	155	190	133	203
1950	168	174	252	169	292
1960	290	282	343	219	381
1970	442	482	473	301	446

SOURCE: E. H. Phelps Brown, "Levels and Movements of Industrial Productivity and Real Wages Internationally Compared, 1860–1970," *Economic Journal* 83 (March 1973): 58–71; see Tables 3 and 5 of his Appendix.
NOTE: As stressed in footnote 12, above, these wages indexes cannot exactly be correlated with hourly wages in the United States based on Rees's estimates as given in Tables 7–10.

ilar in terms of increases in the value of human time to that described for the United States; and (5) it may be presumed that the observed behavior of value and prices is a consequence of a particular type of economic growth.

Before entering upon explanations, however, there is one additional set of special prices to bear in mind, namely the prices of the commodities that are most closely identified with natural resources. It is useful to see them over time because of the widely held belief that natural resources are the critical limiting factor in the economy. Table 12 gives these prices both for renewable natural resources—in agriculture and forestry—and for nonrenewable natural resources—mining, including mineral fuels. The commodity prices are, of course, not pure natural-resource service prices; far from it, for they also incorporate, in various combinations, the productive services of labor, the price of which has been rising, and of reproducible material capital.

Most of the natural-resource commodities tend to remain

Table 12 INDEXES OF DEFLATED NATURAL RESOURCE COMMODITY PRICES, UNITED STATES, 1900–1972 (1900 = 100)

Year	All Commodities	All Agriculture	All Crops	All Livestock	All Forestry	All Metals	All Mineral Fuels	Bituminous Coal	Petroleum	Natural Gas
1900	100	100	100	100	100	100	100	100	100	(100)
1910	99	126	118	127	99	76	48	93	42	118
1920	109	111	87	118	97	66	118	146	131	114
1930	76	90	73	99	56	45	61	79	59	80
1940	77	86	73	95	87	60	59	104	57	68
1950	108	131	110	141	99	68	81	156	84	119
1960	87	95	75	101	90	75	79	125	79	111
1970	79	88	66	100	74	76	72	125	68	111
1972	83	92	69	104	84	71	73	143	67	112

SOURCES: Neal Potter and Francis T. Christy, Jr., *Trends in Natural Resource Commodities* (Baltimore: Johns Hopkins University Press for Resources for the Future, 1962). Actual prices are weighted by the value of output, updated using 1967 weights by Robert S. Manthy, Michigan State University. The indexes of actual prices are deflated by the Consumer Price Index (1967 = 100).

fairly constant over time in their physical, chemical, or biological attributes. A bushel of wheat produced in 1900 differed very little from a bushel produced in 1970; and the same was true of a ton of lead, copper, or sulphur. Quality changes occur, however, in milk and in other livestock products, for example. The historical records of these commodity prices are in general more reliable than those for intermediate goods. For the United States, we have an excellent study by Potter and Christy of commodities produced by extractive industries.[13] The Potter-Christy estimates have been updated by Manthy.[14]

What Table 12 shows is that the trend of the deflated natural resource commodity prices over this period was slightly downward, compared to the more than fivefold rise in real hourly wages shown in Table 7.[15] In agriculture, the deflated prices of *crops* declined about a third, despite various government price supports during parts of this period; the index for *livestock* closed at the level at which it began. In general, the costs of producing livestock products have been affected more by the increase in the price of human time than have the costs of producing crops. The deflated prices of mineral fuels indicate that whereas the deflated price index for all mineral fuels was about a fourth less at the end of this period compared to 1900, the price of bituminous coal rose and that of petroleum fell. It is undoubtedly true that the rise in real wages accounts for a good deal in the increase in coal prices.[16]

13. Neal Potter and Francis T. Christy, Jr., *Trends in Natural Resource Commodities* (Baltimore: Johns Hopkins Press for Resources for the Future, 1962).

14. Professor Robert S. Manthy of Michigan State University has been most generous in making offsets of his numerous tables available to me. I am much indebted to him.

15. No doubt the reader, being strongly of the belief that the 1973–75 upsurge in the prices of the services most dependent on natural resources was the beginning of a new era, will be inclined to look upon the indexes of prices in this table as bygones that are no longer meaningful. The argument against this view is that the events, both natural and man-made, that have accounted for the current upsurge are in large part transitory.

16. For a more complete analysis of these commodity prices and of natural resource rents, see my essay on this topic in *Lectures in Agricultural*

EXPLANATION

Without a useful theory, there can be no satisfactory analysis of the determinants that account for the changes in relative prices that have been presented. The determinants are presumably an integral part of the historical process covered in the preceding section. Since "growth" implies changes over time, the theory that is required could be referred to as a theory of economic growth. But it is fair to say that, as yet, there is no growth theory that is sufficiently comprehensive in specifying the factors and events that determine the changes in relative prices and stocks of resources that occur as a consequence of observable economic behavior and that are in turn consistent with that behavior. Early classical economics was much concerned about prices, but not about the turn that the prices or rents of the services of the factors of production have taken in the countries here under consideration. Meanwhile, modern macro-growth theory has tended to concentrate on changes in resource quantities.

There is little that is analytically useful in the various classical controversies that bear on the prices before us. The history of the price effects of natural-resource rents on growth and income shares is not at home in Ricardian rent. In fact, the rent share and the economic and associated social and political importance of landlords have declined markedly over time in high-income countries. Once again, why has Ricardian rent lost its economic sting in these countries? The controversy over the Malthusian tendency toward subsistence wages provides no real clues to the factors and the process that may have accounted for the present high levels of living of the rank and file of working people in the countries in question. What is called for instead is a population-equilibrium theory that is determined by the high

Economics, bicentennial year lectures sponsored by the USDA Economic Research Service (Washington, D.C.: USDA, June 1977); see also John V. Krutilla and Anthony C. Fisher, *The Economics of the Natural Environment* (Baltimore: Johns Hopkins University Press for Resources for the Future, 1975); and Peter H. Lindert, "Land Scarcity and American Growth," *Journal of Economic History* 34 (1974): 851–84.

value of human time.[17] Nor do exploitation-of-labor polemics, coupled with Marx's argument that wages tend to a subsistence level because of the industrial reserve army of unemployed workers, throw any light on the reasons for the large increases in real wages which require illumination. Although the magnificent classical dynamics gives much attention to prices and wages, it is not oriented to deal with our problem.

A simple supply-and-demand approach helps to clarify matters. It is the intercept of the supply of and the demand for human time that reveals the price we observe. Shifts in the supply and demand schedules then account for the recorded increases in this price over time. The key to this pricing problem is in the factors that determine such shifts. We know a good deal about the factors that increase the *supply*, both in terms of the size of the labor force and of the quality attributes of the workers. But this is at best a partial picture of the price changes that occur. The nub of the unresolved problem is that we know very little about the factors that shift the *demand* upward over time so strongly.

In devising an approach to get at the factors that explain the shifts in these two schedules, *an all-inclusive concept of capital formation is necessary*. In using this concept, it is essential to see the heterogeneity of the various old and new forms of capital and to specify them in sufficient detail to determine not only the substitutions but also the interacting complementarity between these forms of capital. Inasmuch as capital formation entails investment, it is important not to conceal the changes over time in incentives—that is, the anticipated rates of return to be had from alternative investment.

Changes in investment opportunities, events, and human behavior alter the scale of value and the composition of the stock of capital. Alterations that enhance the scope of

17. See Theodore W. Schultz, "Fertility and Economic Values, II. The High Value of Human Time: Population Equilibrium," pp. 14–22, and Marc Nerlove, "Toward a New Theory of Population and Economic Growth," pp. 527–45, in *Economics of the Family: Marriage, Children, and Human Capital*, ed. Theodore W. Schultz (Chicago: University of Chicago Press, 1974).

choices are favorable developments. The various forms of capital differ significantly in their attributes. Natural resources are not reproducible, but structures, equipment, and inventories of commodities and goods are. Human beings are productive agents with the attributes of human capital, and they are also the optimizing agents. In a fundamental sense, it is their preferences that matter in the use that is made of the various forms of capital. It is noteworthy that in high-income countries the rate at which human capital increases exceeds that of nonhuman capital.

In specifying the heterogeneity of capital, it is not sufficient to classify the capital forms as natural resources, reproducible material forms, and human capital, because of the important role that new forms of capital within each of these classes play in altering relative prices (returns) and in shifting supply and demand schedules. An all-inclusive concept of capital that accounts fully for its heterogeneity is the core of the analytical model that is required.[18] It will be necessary to make room in this approach to growth and changes in relative prices for the following three propositions:

(1) The Ricardian principle that an increasing share of national income accrues to land rent (natural resources) needs to be replaced by the proposition that this share tends to decline as a consequence of man-made substitutes for land. A notable example is the creation of hybrid corn, which may be viewed either as a substitute or as a new input augmenting the yield from land. Plastics and aluminum become substitutes for various metals and wood; and nuclear energy becomes a substitute for fossil fuels. The economics of producing such substitutes (research and development) is still in its infancy, and the prospective output of this sector is subject to the same uncertainty as are other advances in useful knowledge.

(2) Some new forms of capital complement other forms of capital in production. A consequence of such complemen-

18. See Harry G. Johnson, "Toward a Generalized Capital Accumulation Approach to Economic Development," in *The Residual Factor and Economic Growth* (Paris: OECD, 1964), pp. 219–27.

tarity is that particular new forms of material capital increase the demand for particular human skills (a subclass of human capital). A recent example of this is the computer. In turn, new forms of human capital increase the demand for additional material capital of a particular sort. The development of an intricate bacteriological method for controlling airborne fungi while introducing desired flavor-augmenting bacteria in producing cheeses and other milk products—a method that required the skill of a Ph.D. in a branch of bacteriology—increased the demand for Ph.D.'s qualified to use this method and the demand for new types of equipment on the part of dairy industry. These complementary forms of capital need to be identified and included in the analytical model.

(3) Making room in economic growth models for changes in relative prices over time is a return to the approach of early classical economics. Since modern macro-growth models tend to take prices as given (usually fixed), the inclusion of relative prices and their function is a radical analytical proposition. Be that as it may, relative prices, which include the alternative rates of return on investment, are the mainspring that drives the economic system. If this mainspring did not exist, we would have to invent it by appealing to shadow prices.

The shifts in demand in favor of productive services of labor that contribute to increases in the price of human time are, in large part, a consequence of the complementarity proposed in the second of these propositions. But the state of the art of economics does not as yet permit us to identify and determine the effects of this complementarity on the demand for labor.

The price and income effects of increases in the value of human time include enlargement of institutional protection of the rights of workers, favoring human capital relative to property rights; increases in the value added by labor, relative to that added by materials in production; a decline in hours worked; increases in labor's share of national income;

a decline in fertility; and the high rate at which human capital increases. The human agent becomes ever more a capitalist by virtue of his personal human capital, and he seeks political support to protect the value of that capital. The rise in the value of human time makes new demands on institutions. Some political and legal institutions are especially subject to these demands. What we observe is that these institutions respond in many ways. The legal rights of labor are enlarged and in the process some of the rights of property are curtailed. The legal rights of tenants are also enhanced. Seniority and safety at work receive increasing protection.[19] The history of national income by type indicates clearly that large changes have occurred over time that parallel, and are associated with, a rise in the real earnings of workers. The interactions between the labor force at work and hourly wages on the one hand and the amount of nonhuman capital and the price of the services of that capital on the other are exceedingly complex. Kuznets gives us an analysis of these interactions, in which he takes account of the increases in the stock of wealth represented by "land," of the stock of reproducible producer capital, and the changes in the prices of the services of these forms of capital, along with the increases in the total man-hours worked and the rise in the price per man-hour worked.[20] His analysis implies a large relative increase in the value added by labor.

The obverse of the increase in labor's contribution to national income is the decline in the share contributed by property assets. Kuznets takes a fairly long view of this development in Western countries, finding that the share of

19. See my "Institutions and the Rising Economic Value of Man," *American Journal of Agricultural Economics* 50 (December 1968), pp. 1113–22. Also see the useful paper by Vernon W. Ruttan, *Integrated Rural Development Programs: A Skeptical Perspective* (Agricultural Development Council, New York, 1975), reprinted from *International Development Review* 17, no. 4 (1975).

20. See Simon Kuznets, *Modern Economic Growth* (New Haven: Yale University Press, 1966), pp. 181–83, which bears directly on this analytical issue. This part of the analysis is restricted to the United States and to the period from 1909–14 to 1955–57.

national income attributed to property assets declined from about 45 to 25 percent, while labor's part rose from about 55 to 75 percent.[21]

By 1970, about three-fourths of the official U.S. national income by type consisted of employee compensation.[22] The remaining fourth is classified as proprietors' income, rental income, net interest, and corporate profits. These four classes of "property" income include considerable earnings[23] that accrue to human agents for the productive time they devote to self-employed work and to the management of their property assets. A conservative estimate of the aggregate contribution of human agents in 1970, measured by employee compensation, plus self-employment earnings and management of assets within the domain of the market sector, was fully four-fifths of the value of the production accounted for in national income.

Measured national income, however, is substantially less than the full income that people realize from the services of their property and from their time, inasmuch as the concept of national income is restricted to the economic activities of the market sector. It excludes the economic value of all household production. The additional income that is realized from household production is, in large part, contributed

21. Simon Kuznets's studies of economic growth and the distribution of income are classic contributions to this subject. See, in addition to *Modern Economic Growth*, his "Economic Growth and Income Inequality," *American Economic Review* 45 (March 1955): 1–28; "Quantitative Aspects of the Economic Growth of Nations: VIII. Distribution of Income by Size," *Economic Development and Cultural Change* 11, no. 2, pt. 2 (January 1963): 1–80; and *Economic Growth and Nations* (Cambridge, Mass.: Harvard University Press, 1971).

22. *Long Term Economic Growth, 1860–1970* (Washington, D.C.: U.S. Bureau of Economic Analysis, 1973), p. 22. Compensation of employees includes income accruing as wages, salaries, tips, bonuses, commissions, vacation pay, and payments in kind. Also included are supplements and fringe benefits such as employer contributions to private pension, health, and welfare funds.

23. We shall restrict the concept of *earnings* to the income that accrues to human agents as compensation for their productive services. The income accruing to the owners of property assets for the productive services of their property will be referred to as *property income*.

by the value of the time of housewives. Also omitted is the value of time that adult students invest in their education, and the partially compensated time that younger members of the labor force invest in on-the-job training. These, and still other income-producing activities, are not included in the accounting of national income.

The price and income effects of hourly earnings explain a wide array of changes in the allocation of time. When expected future earnings from more education rise, the response of youth is to postpone work for pay in order to devote more years to education. The advantage of youth in acquiring additional education is twofold: the wages foregone are lower than they would be later, and there are more years ahead to cash in on the anticipated higher earnings and satisfactions. As wages increase, people who earn their income by working can afford to retire at an earlier age because of the larger retirement income that they are able to accumulate. This is counterbalanced by the improvement in health that is purchased, which extends the years that individuals may opt to work. The rise in the value of the time of women is an incentive to substitute various forms of physical capital in household production, and, inasmuch as children are labor-intensive for women, the demand for children is reduced, and an increasing part of women's time is allocated to the labor market.

The increases in earnings also explain the decline in hours of work or the increase in leisure during this century. For the U.S. civilian economy, the average weekly hours worked declined from about 53 to 37 over the period from 1900 to 1970, and the average annual hours worked per employee decreased from 2,766 to 1,929. The interaction between annual hours allocated to work and earnings shows a decline of 7 percent in hours and a 43 percent increase in annual earnings between 1900 and 1920; for the 1920 to 1940 period these changes were 12 percent and 53 percent respectively; and for 1940 to 1970 annual hours declined 13 percent, while real annual earnings increased by 73 percent.[24]

24. See Appendix: Table C for the data on which the figures in this paragraph are based.

The employed civilian labor force in the United States was 26.96 million in 1900, and 78.63 million in 1970, but when adjustment is made for the 30 percent decline in annual hours worked, the increase in total employed hours in 1970 is only twice that of 1900. Despite the decline in annual hours, aggregate labor earnings in 1967 dollars were slightly more than eleven times as large in 1970 as they were in 1900. The distribution of U.S. national income by type implies a somewhat larger aggregate for the earnings of labor in 1970, however, the plausible explanation being that the real wage of manufacturing workers understates somewhat the average annual earnings of the employed labor force, as would be expected in view of the relatively large increase in the number of better-educated salaried workers.

Another approach is to examine the changes in the functional shares of the various types of national income. During the 1900–1909 period, using the official concept of national income, employee compensation accounted for about 55 percent, compared to 75 percent in 1970.[25] Between 1909 and 1970, the changes in the shares of income other than employee compensation were as follows: proprietors' income declined from about 24 to 8 percent, rental income from 9 to 3 percent, and net interest from 5.5 to 4.1 percent, whereas corporate profits rose from 7 to 9 percent. The latter two income components fluctuated widely over this period, as would be expected in view of the uneven performance of the economy.

Lastly we turn to the investment in human capital.[26] Economic theory has in recent years been extended to explain the accumulation of human capital, and the price and income effects of this form of capital. The theory has led to

25. *Long Term Economic Growth, 1860–1970*, p. 22, gives percent distribution of national income by type.

26. For a generalized approach to this type of investment, see my "Investment in Human Capital," *American Economic Review* 51 (March 1961), pp. 1–17; see also, *Human Resources*, NBER Fiftieth Anniversary Colloquium VI (New York: National Bureau of Economic Research, 1972); *The Economic Value of Education* (New York: Columbia University Press, 1963); and *Investment in Human Capital: The Role of Education and Research* (New York: Free Press, 1971).

important new approaches in bringing economics to bear on human behavior.[27]

As already noted, although the U.S. labor force virtually tripled between 1900 and 1970, the aggregate hours devoted to market work increased much less, as a consequence of the decreases in annual hours worked. During this same period, however, the aggregate stock of education embodied in the U.S. labor force, measured in terms of 1956 unit costs of education, increased from 63 billion to 815 billion dollars, a thirteenfold increase. Estimates of the costs of education for selected years from 1900 to 1957 were published in 1961.[28]

The first important calculation in these estimates of the costs of education is adjustment for changes in the level of prices. For the base price year 1956, per capita costs come to $280 per annum for elementary schooling, $1,420 per year for high school, and $3,300 per annum for college and university education. A second calculation entails adjusting the figures for elementary schooling to an *equivalent school year* of 152 days of school attendance to cope with the fact that starting with 1900 the average attendance of enrolled pupils aged five to fifteen was only 99 days. Table 13 shows the years of schooling and the costs of this schooling per member of the labor force for 1900, 1940, 1957, and 1970.

Whereas human-capital accounting includes investment in on-the-job training, which is large, as Mincer has shown, the costs and returns of migration, and investments made to improve health, education is probably the most important factor in this context.[29] The increases in the value of educa-

27. See, especially, the seminal contributions of Gary S. Becker, which include *Human Capital: A Theoretical and Empirical Analysis with Special Reference to Education* (New York: National Bureau of Economic Research, 1964); "A Theory of the Allocation of Time," *Economic Journal* 75 (September 1963): 493–517; "A Theory of Marriage," in the *Economics of the Family*, ed. Schultz, pp. 299–344; and *The Economic Approach to Human Behavior, Schooling, Experience and Earnings* (New York: National Bureau of Economic Research and Columbia University Press, 1974).

28. See my "Education and Economic Growth," in *Social Forces Influencing American Education*, ed. Nelson B. Henry (Chicago: University of Chicago Press, 1961), pp. 46–86.

29. See Jacob Mincer, "On-the-Job Training: Costs, Returns, and Some Implications," pp. 50–79, and Larry A. Sjaastad, "The Costs and Returns of

Year	Level of Schooling	(1) Years of School per capita[a]	(2) Cost per Year in 1956 Prices	(3) Cost per Member of Labor Force (Col. 1 × Col. 2)	(4) Percentage Distribution of Col. 3
1900	Elementary	3.437	$ 280	$ 962	43
	High School	0.556	1420	790	35
	College and University	0.147	3300	485	22
	TOTAL	4.140		2237	100
1940	Elementary	6.85	280	1918	33
	High School	1.71	1420	2428	41
	College and University	0.46	3300	1518	26
	TOTAL	9.02		5864	100
1957	Elementary	7.52	280	2106	28
	High School	2.44	1420	3458	45
	College and University	0.64	3300	2099	27
	TOTAL	10.60		7663	100
1970	Elementary	7.75	280	2170	23
	High School	3.04	1420	4317	45
	College and University	.91	3300	3003	32
	TOTAL	11.70		9490	100

SOURCES: The estimates for 1900, 1940, and 1957 appear in my "Education and Economic Growth," cited above, Tables 11, 12, and 13. Those for 1970 were undertaken for this paper. The official data on median years of schooling overstate the actual years as shown in this table. No upward adjustment has been made for the fact that the average number of days of school attendance had risen to 163 by 1970.
[a] Adjusted for school attendance.

tion in the U.S. labor force, based on the costs of acquiring the education, add to the stock of human capital relative to the stock of reproducible nonhuman capital, which is shown for selected years from 1900 to 1970 in Table 14.

Throughout most of the world, labor still earns a pittance. Countries with low earnings cover most of the world's map. In a few countries, however, the value of the time of working people is exceedingly high. The high price of human time that characterizes these exceptional countries is, from the viewpoint of economic history, a recent development. In these countries, the increases in real wages and salaries represent gains in economic welfare which are the most significant achievement of their economic growth. Much less time is allocated to work for pay. Most of the work is no longer hard physically. Ever more skills are demanded, and the supply response of skills is strong and clear. But the increases in demand are still concealed in the complementarity between the various new forms of capital. On human-capital formation, Kuznets's telling remarks open the door.

[Some] components now included under consumption could be viewed as capital investment, not because the expenditure is on durable goods . . . but because the use of the good is closely related to the efficiency of the consumer as a producer. The main item in question is the outlays on education (formal and on-the-job training) and there are some outlays on health care and recreation. . . . These components are far from negligible. . . . If direct costs of formal education alone are over 20 percent of gross capital formation, outlays on education, health, and recreation, treatable as investment in man, may well be as high as four-tenths of capital formation.[30]

The historical fact is that, despite the vast accumulation of capital, the real rate of return on investment has not diminished over time. Almost forty years ago, in one of his classic papers, Knight had already perceived the role of improvements in the quality of the labor force and of the ad-

---

Human Migration," pp. 80–93, in *Investment in Human Beings*, ed. Theodore W. Schultz, a supplement to the *Journal of Political Economy* 70, pt. 2 (October 1962).

30. *Modern Economic Growth*, p. 228.

Table 14 STOCK OF EDUCATION IN THE U.S. LABOR FORCE AND STOCK OF TWO CLASSES OF REPRODUCIBLE NONHUMAN CAPITAL COMPARED FOR SELECTED YEARS, 1900 TO 1970

Year	(1) Educational Stock in Labor Force[a]	(2) Stock of Reproducible Nonhuman Wealth[a]	(3) Col. 1 as Percentage of Col. 2	(4) Stock of Business Capital[a]	(5) Col. 1 as Percentage of Col. 4
1900	63	282	22		
1910	94	463	23		
1920	127	526	24		
1930	180	735	24	491	37
1940	248	756	33	475	52
1950	359	969	37	557	64
1957	535	1270	42	700	76
1970	815			1089	75

SOURCES: Cols. 1 and 2 for 1900 and up through 1957 are from my "Education and Economic Growth," cited above, Table 14. Col. 2 is from Raymond W. Goldsmith, *The National Wealth of the United States in the Postwar Period* (Princeton, N.J.: Princeton University Press, 1962). Col. 4 is from series A 151 in *Long Term Economic Growth, 1860–1970*, cited above, pp. 206–7. In estimating educational stock for 1970, the labor force aged 16 and over is used, whereas for earlier years the reported labor force is that aged 12 and over.
[a] In billions of dollars.

vances in the sciences as they affect the rate of return on investment.[31] There has been much aimless wandering in analyzing growth that could have been avoided had the perceptions of Marshall been heeded.

Capital consists in a great part of knowledge and organization: knowledge is the most powerful engine of production. . . . The distinction between public and private property in knowledge and organization is of great and growing importance: in some respects of more importance than that between public and private property in material things.[32]

Public and private investment in human capital and in useful knowledge are a large part of the story in accounting for the increases in the value of human time.

31. Frank Knight, "Diminishing Returns from Investment," *Journal of Political Economy* 52 (March 1944): 26–47.
32. *Principles of Economics*, bk. 4, pp. 138–39.

When Economic
Distortions Prevail

5
Distortions of Schooling in Large Cities

Many big school systems in our major cities are performing badly. Teachers face distorted incentives. The schooling of the children is inadequate. Educational reforms have become the order of the day. Many parents know that the quality of the schooling their children receive is inadequate, but there is little they can do about it except change their place of residence, or opt for private schools and pay both school taxes and tuition. Clearly, many American children are being undereducated. In large city schools, equity is not being achieved and quality is declining. What has gone wrong in these public schools?

The value of schooling is not in doubt. There is much confusion, however, in taking advantage of what we know about the value of education in solving the present acute problems in schooling. Until we identify the problems clearly and precisely, the prospects of solving them are bleak. Although the concepts of efficiency and equity are relevant for this purpose, they are not sufficient.

Our schooling is overwhelmingly dependent on public funds. Public funds are not free; they are not unencum-

In writing this chapter I have drawn on an article prepared for a book on the financing of education edited by Walter W. McMahon and Terry G. Geske (University of Illinois Press, forthcoming), which deals with important aspects of human capital and the financing of education to a greater extent than the present work. I am indebted to McMahon and Geske for their helpful suggestions.

bered; they are not an unmixed blessing. Public control of how these funds are used is clearly a major problem. Public funding is also unstable. When it increases rapidly, the boom in education results in distortions. When public funds are cut, the educational enterprise is in difficulty. Nor is it clear that more funds would remedy the big-school disease. More funds would not correct the lack of incentive on the part of teachers to improve their performance. More funds will not per se reduce the burden placed on school children by endeavors to use education as an instrument to achieve social reforms; and would tend to reduce further the decision-making authority of parents in respect to schooling.

The complementarity between efficiency and equity in schooling is being overlooked in the quest for equity. An optimum level of efficiency in our big school systems would in all probability contribute more to the cause of equity than any of the many reforms now being imposed.

Education, including university research, has over the years contributed substantially to the productivity of the economy and to welfare. As chapter 4 shows, the total compensation in real terms per hour of work of manufacturing workers, who are the largest part of the labor force, increased more than fivefold between 1900 and 1975. The dynamics of productivity have been such that the rates of return on education have tended over time to exceed the rates of return on physical capital. In response to this difference in returns, the growth in the stock of human capital, consisting largely of education, has been somewhat higher than that of physical capital. The share of income accruing to property has declined from about 45 to 20 percent, whereas the share accruing to labor, broadly defined to include all the human services of the market sector, has risen from about 55 to 80 percent. All of these achievements, however, omit the nonmarket contributions of education in household production, in child care, in the acquisition and maintenance of health, in increasing the ability of consumers to purchase goods and services, in enabling parents to evaluate the quality of the schooling that their children receive, and, most important, in determining social competence and the quality of the style of living. These nonmarket values are omitted in the rates of return to education that are derived from market-sector activities.

Keeping these historical achievements firmly in mind, how do we account for the present trouble in much of our educational system? High-school grades have become increasingly unreliable.[1] Freshmen entering college show higher high-school grades than ever, whereas college test scores are declining.[2] The quality of college instruction in many institutions is declining, and college grades have become inflated. A *Science* editorial asks, "Can Meritocracy In Academe Be Saved?"[3] Universities are being seriously impaired by increasing governmental intervention and sanctions. Universities are not defending their true function, however; they have, in the words of Edward Shils, become too fond of Caesar.[4]

The convenience of deficit financing of education is no longer assured. It is a serious setback for school finances that property taxes are being frozen or sharply reduced, as has occurred in California. To the extent that local schools still have some political autonomy, it is largely a function of revenue from local property taxes. In fact, once the effects of real estate taxes are accounted for in the capitalization of land values, the rents paid for the services of the land are in general very little altered. Yet publicly we are bent on reducing taxes on real estate, the land component in homes, and on land generally, although the prices of land have risen substantially more than the rate of inflation.

No individual can sell his educational capital; nor is it

1. John Walsh, "Does High School Grade Inflation Mask a More Alarming Trend?" *Science*, March 9, 1979, p. 982.

2. Alexander W. Astin, Margo R. King, and Gerald T. Richardson, *The American Freshman: Norms for Fall, 1978* (Los Angeles: University of California Graduate School of Education, 1979).

3. *Science*, March 23, 1979, p. 1199. An editorial attributed to John D. Palmer, chairman of the Department of Zoology, University of Massachusetts, Amherst.

4. Edward Shils, "The Conflict of God and Caesar," the second of three 1979 Jefferson Lectures, presented at the University of Chicago, April 10, 1979.

possible for him to transfer the stock of education that he possesses as a gift to someone else. It is his stock of human capital, to use and to keep as long as he lives. Physical capital, which still dominates our thinking, differs markedly in important respects. Private ownership of physical capital is governed by property rights. Such property can be sold; it can be transferred as a gift to others. Factories, equipment, homes, and inventories can be destroyed. Private property is subject to annual taxation, to inheritance taxation, and may be confiscated by governments. During World War II, the stock of human capital in Germany and Japan, despite casualties, was much less impaired than the stock of physical capital. Refugees take their human capital with them when they flee. Walls are built to make it impossible for people to flee; emigration can be prohibited. Even so, in the extreme, governments cannot confiscate human capital, although they can destroy its value.

The production and consumption services of human and physical capital have many economic attributes in common. At many points in ongoing economic activities they are complementary, and they are also substitutes for each other. Highly skilled labor is essential in many types of modern economic activity. Physical capital is often a substitute for labor; farm tractors reduce the labor that is required. Modern large tractors, however, require skilled operators.

Economists concerned about human capital have been all too silent on the political implications of their contributions. Americans proclaim their liberal values and democratic institutions, and human values are deemed to be fundamental. Consistent with these values, our government does not build walls to keep educated people from leaving the United States; but, inconsistently, we erect fences to keep people out, and mandate selective immigration quotas, though we occasionally allow in particular refugees.

Public policy that minimizes the authority of parents in determining the quality of the schooling their children receive is also clearly inconsistent with liberal values. Within the private market sector, which still accounts for most of the formation of physical capital, entrepreneurs decide the specifications of the investment they will undertake and the amount that they will invest. Parents who have children in big-city schools, on the other hand, can do very little to determine the specifications of the schooling their children receive. This is all the more incongruous in view of the impressive rise in the education of parents. Parents have the option of moving to the suburbs, and many are doing so; but to entertain the idea of the families of the million elementary and high-school students in the New York City school system all moving into suburbia is to contemplate a nightmare.

This unsatisfactory state of affairs is largely a consequence of the ever deeper wedge separating both basic schooling and higher education from the self-interest of parents and students. The separation is most acute in elementary and secondary schooling, especially so in the big school systems. The educational investment that matters is that in acquired ability. Although the self-interest of parents and their children is fundamental to the success of organized education, it is ever more excluded because of the way education is financed, organized, and administered. We have invented four reasons for reducing the authority of parents:

(1) The technology and subject matter of schooling is now largely determined by professional educators and school administrators. Classroom teachers are deemed to be unqualified in this respect, as are parents, regardless of how well they may be educated. They are told—and even that is largely a matter of public relations.

(2) There is a political belief, shared by some professional educators, that big school systems have a comparative advantage in providing the essential components of quality instruction.

(3) It is a long-standing concern of most educational finance experts to achieve equality in funds per pupil. The process of achieving this objective has undoubtedly contributed much to the centralization of educational decisions. The funding of education has been shifted ever more from local sources to state and federal ones. In 1929–30, about 83

percent of U.S. public elementary and secondary school revenue came from local sources, and almost none from the federal government. By 1977–78, local revenue had declined to slightly less than 48 percent, while federal funds accounted for 8 percent and state funds for 44 percent. The control of education has likewise shifted, which should have been anticipated, knowing as we do that he who pays the piper calls the tune. It is a critical error to overlook this centralizing of control, although there are hypothetically ways to hold it in abeyance (for example, general-purpose grants that would avoid central control). Clearly this has not been done, as is evident from the strong tendency of the federal and state governments to mandate how schools are to be administered. Over time, the management of schools shifted in favor of school superintendents and school boards, and then to city-wide administrators. They, in turn, became beholden to state superintendents of education, and all are now in the domain of accountability and subject to the regulations of the federal government.

(4) Education is deemed to be one of the major instruments in achieving social reforms. In terms of accountability, all parts of our educational system, not only elementary and secondary schools but also colleges and universities, are required by law to be active agents of reform. The social objectives are consistent with widely held values, and the attainment of some of these objectives is long overdue. The unsettled questions are: Is education an effective instrument in achieving these reforms? Are the changes in education that have been mandated appropriate means of attaining these social objectives? To what extent is the quality of education altered by such means?

To the extent that parents and teachers are bound to the existing school organization, and to the way it is financed and controlled, what can they do to improve the human capital that their children acquire from their schooling? Consider the mammoth school system of New York City. What can the parents of any of the one million children enrolled in public elementary and secondary schools, or any of the more than fifty thousand classroom teachers in the New

York City system, actually do individually to improve it? Frank J. Macchiarola, who has recently been appointed to administer the New York City school system, is by all accounts an exceedingly competent public administrator. But what can he do that would make that system perform efficiently?[5] The answer is obvious, it seems to me: it simply cannot be done by any one individual, given the financial structure, the public sources of control, and the inordinate size of the system.

Teachers are much maligned. It is said they are not concerned about the educational achievements of their students. In the large school systems, they join and establish strong teachers' unions. Through them, they bargain for "less instructional time, less extracurriculum involvement, greater reliance upon union contracts as the standards of professional responsibility,"[6] better facilities, more fringe benefits, and promotion and school assignment formulas that will serve their self-interest. They are said to show little or no interest in improving the quality of their teaching. My argument is that most of this might have been anticipated in view of the way schools are organized and administered. Neither the curriculum, the promotion and the permissible discipline of students, nor the objectives of the courses to be taught are for teachers to decide. These decisions are placed in the domain of professional educators. In assessing performance it is a dictum of economics that incentives matter, but the incentives to become an excellent teacher have become weak and ambiguous; furthermore, they are badly distorted. School teachers are responding to the greatly circumscribed opportunities open to them as

5. See Macchiarola's 24-page "Mid-Year Report of the Chancellor of the Schools for New York City Board of Education" (January 1979). In the first seven pages "accountability" is stressed fourteen times; also featured are "the immense and far-flung bureaucracy," the "proliferation of fraudulent academic courses," the "situation of waste," and the "rip-off" by bus contractors. "Society has turned against children," Macchiarola asserts. "We are sorely mistaken if we believe that increased funding provides a solution to the problem of lack of commitment." He adds that "the management task is enormous" [I would have said *impossible*].

6. Ibid., p. 11.

should be expected. They are not robots; they are human agents who perceive, interpret, and act in accordance with the worthwhile options available to them.

I do not condone the widespread poor performance of many teachers in the big school systems. Like organized construction workers, organized teachers exact a high toll. My argument is that these teachers are responding to the organization and administration of vastly overlarge systems. It certainly is true, however, that teachers did not create them. Professional educators, public finance experts and the politics of education are the architects of these highly inefficient school systems.

One-teacher schools have become a curiosity, though in my youth there were more of them than all the other public schools. Professional educators promoted consolidation, and they succeeded politically. Ever more consolidation became a compelling objective. Since 1931–32, the number of school districts has been reduced from 127,000 to 16,000, and public elementary schools from 233,000 to 63,000, whereas nonpublic elementary schools have increased from 9,000 to 14,000. As of 1976, there were 188 public school systems, each with an enrollment of 25,000 or more children. They accounted for 28 percent of all enrolled children in public schools and averaged over 66,000 students per system. The saddest part of this story is in the size of the school systems in the twenty large cities of the United States for which data are readily available.[7] Nor have colleges and universities been immune. As of 1976, there were no less than 40 U.S. college and university campuses with enrollments of over 25,000 students.[8]

The supply of rhetoric about efficiency in education is very large. The supply of competent studies of efficiency in education is minuscule. In determining the efficiency of any school system in producing educational services, we must ascertain the economics of the scale of that system. The analytical task is neither simple nor easy, but the costs of the

---

7. See *Digest of Education Statistics 1977–78* (Washington, D.C.: National Center for Education Statistics, 1978), Table 36.

8. Ibid., Table 78.

services that enter into education and the value of the services that are produced depend in no small part on the scale of the educational enterprise.

What we have is rarely the optimum scale. Although I do not believe that small is necessarily beautiful, and it can be expensive, the belief that *bigger is better* must be challenged. The review of the sparse literature and the conclusions of Sher and Tompkins, who find that the premise that supports the widely accepted view that "bigger is better" is untenable, are a useful contribution.[9]

We have evolved a public school system that has literally acquired the economic attributes of a company store. Most parents are bound by residence to the school district in which they live. Like serfs in old Russia, they can purchase their freedom, but the price is very high. Enrolling children in a private school means paying both the taxes that support public schools and high tuition. Nor are all private schools free of religious and racial overtones and readily accessible. To the extent that public schools in different locations differ in quality, some families will pay the price of relocating. The movement out of the school systems of large cities into those of adjacent suburbs is clear evidence of this. Taking up residence in a suburb is no assurance, however, that one's children will not be bussed back to city schools.

There is frequent reference in the literature on education to participation and involvement on the part of parents and students. These concepts appear to have no precise operational specifications, but vague and ambiguous as they are, I have found few calls for delegation to parents of a modicum of authority over any part of school affairs. Such a delegation of power would, in fact, violate the legal authority under which most large city schools operate and are administered.[10] It is in this important sense that public school systems have the economic attributes of a monopoly, more so than a company store. School attendance is compulsory, and

9. Jonathan P. Sher and Rachel B. Tompkins, "Economy, Efficiency and Equality" (Washington, D.C.: National Institute of Education, July 1976).

10. For a useful study, see Dale Mann, *The Politics of Administrative Representation* (Lexington, Mass.: Lexington Books, 1976).

children and parents as individuals must accept this schooling, however bad it may be, unless they can afford the cost of
changing their residence or making double payments by opt-
ing for a private school.

To approach public education as I have done here may appear to beg two questions. Are parents competent to determine the quality of schooling? Are they willing privately to
support the reforms that the politics of education has mandated? It is to be regretted that the old controversy over the
competence of parents on matters pertaining to education is
no longer with us. Professional educators, with the support
of experts in public finance and of government, have won
the verdict that parents are not sufficiently competent to
judge the technical requirements of schooling, the efficiency of classroom and in-school activities, and the quality
of the schooling that their children obtain. It should not
come as a surprise that a formidable array of special interests, both within and outside of these school systems, have
acquired a strong, vested self-interest in maintaining the existing public elementary and secondary school monopoly.

The baneful notion that parents as a class are neither
qualified nor responsible human agents when it comes to
the schooling of their children must be challenged. It is inconsistent with the economic behavior of parents both as a
group and as individuals in many other activities. The implications of human-capital theory and appeal to the evidence to determine the validity of these implications reveal
that parents are competent, calculating human agents. This
is evident in household production, in the marriage market,
in the behavior of women in deciding between household
work and work in the labor force, in the substitution of quality for quantity of children, in investment in the health and
schooling of children, and in other contexts. A decade and a
half ago I challenged the then widely held view that cultiva-
tors in low-income countries were creatures of habit who
were indifferent to any and all new technical and economic
opportunities that might improve their lot.[11] As I argued in

11. See my *Transforming Traditional Agriculture* (New Haven, Conn.:
Yale University Press, 1964; repr. New York: Arno Press, 1976).

chapter 2, parents in low-income countries are not indifferent to opportunities to improve the health of their children and acquire more schooling for them. The evidence which clearly shows that there is a strong private demand by them for health services and schooling for their children has been overlooked. That parents in this country, who are in general better educated than any earlier generation of parents, are incompetent with regard to the education of their children is, in my view, a patently false notion.

The question of social reforms is beset with difficulties. Elements of a public policy to reduce inequality in the personal distribution of income were authorized as long ago as 1913 by a constitutional amendment that legalized progressive income taxation, and public transfers of income to the poor have become very large. There is a clear public interest in protecting civil rights and eliminating various forms of discrimination in order to equalize the opportunities of disadvantaged racial and ethnic groups and of women. But whereas some of the public programs mandated to achieve social reforms have proven to be appropriate and effective (for example, the civil rights protection of blacks in the South in exercising their right to vote), other programs appear to be inappropriate for achieving their social objectives. Some may well be counterproductive, among them reform programs imposed on school systems and institutions of higher education, which fail to achieve their objectives because many parents[12] perceive that they actually reduce the quality of education that their children receive. Inasmuch as most parents place a high value on this quality, they strongly resist such mandated programs.

The inference could be, however, that these parents are opposed to the social objectives that have called forth such programs. How much validity is to be attributed to this is

12. It is all too convenient to believe that it is only high-income families who are concerned about quality in this context. Although the controversy continues, there is an increasing body of evidence, which federal agencies are bent on discrediting, that implies that school busing has not provided quality schooling for blacks. Moreover, an increasing number of black families are perceiving that this is the case.

hard to tell. An alternative inference is that many parents believe that these programs are counterproductive, and that they will not sacrifice the education of their children to accommodate them. There is, however, a more serious issue, which can be stated very bluntly: will society long condone having children used as hostages to obtain compliance? The harassment of superintendents of school systems by withholding federal and state funds and by taking them to court is tolerable. So is the mandated assignment of teachers. But to place children in jeopardy as a means to achieve whatever the objectives are is not tolerable in a civilized society.

The poor schooling that many children in our major cities are receiving does not square with the "overeducated American" thesis. Although it is useful to examine the various trade-offs between efficiency and equity, it is more important not to overlook the complementarity between them in elementary and secondary schooling. Efficient schools would substantially reduce the inequity that now prevails, because in general it is true that the children of the most disadvantaged families are shortchanged most seriously by the existing inefficiency of our school systems. School reforms that would bring about at least an approximately optimum level of efficiency in schools would in all probability contribute more to the cause of equity than any of the various trade-off schemes.

The inefficiency on which I have concentrated is predominantly a consequence of the monopoly that is vested in the public schools, which are effectively sheltered from competition. The question is whether competition would impair the essential public interest in education. Experience in higher education indicates that the answer is in the negative. I doubt that anyone would argue that the 65 private universities and the remaining 1,266 other four-year private institutions of higher education do not serve the public interest.[13] The politics of education is, however, strongly in-

13. See *Digest of Education Statistics 1977–78*, Table 108; the statistics are for 1976–77. See also *A Classification of Institutions of Higher Educa-*

fluenced by organized groups who have a vested interest in keeping competition out of schooling.

A new generation of architects is needed to devise educational policies that will provide parents and their children with options to acquire better schooling. The economic requirements are, in principle, simple: competition would bring about greater efficiency; parents and youth would demand better education. Public funds could be allocated to them, leaving them free to choose their school with no strings attached except that such funds be used for education.[14] Educational subsidies under the G.I. Bill of Rights gave proof that this principle is also applicable to higher education.

What are the prospects? The politics of education in Washington, in the states, and in the location-specific school systems are not immune to change. Our political institutions tend to respond, albeit with a lag, to the changes in public demand for both quantity and quality of education. On this score, optimism is warranted in the long view. But our inability as economists or educators to comprehend the serious limitations of the existing organization, administration, and public financing of basic schooling and higher education lends support to a more pessimistic outlook.

I reject the arguments that all children must be protected from incompetent and malevolent parents, that teachers are to blame for what has gone wrong in schooling, that highly competent school administrators are the solution, that schools must be the agents of social reform regardless of the adverse effects of education, and that competition in the domain of schooling is fundamentally bad.

---

tion (Berkeley, Calif.: Carnegie Commission on Higher Education, 1973), Table 1.

14. I am not featuring the voucher proposal at this point, despite its many merits. There are alternative approaches and the underlying basis for the inefficiency and inequity of schooling must be fully comprehended before any new approach will be taken seriously in the politics of education.

6
Distortions of Research

The validity of Alfred Marshall's perception that "knowledge is the most powerful engine of production" is not in doubt. Advances in knowledge enhance the quality of both physical and human capital. Organized research has become the primary source of additions to the stock of knowledge. Basic research is done in large part within universities; the results of this research are public goods that are placed in the public domain. University research is not a profit-making enterprise. If such research is to be had, it must be supported by public funds and private gifts. In the United States, about 70 percent of all basic science research is paid for by the federal government, and about 60 percent of this research is done by universities and their affiliates. Relations between the federal government and universities have deteriorated greatly during the past decade, however. Academic scientists have become increasingly burdened by government regulations, and economic research is even more vulnerable to these.

Basic research in the sciences has experienced a long boom since World War II. A useful measure of this boom and of the research achievements of the United States is the number of American scientists who have been awarded No-

My first endeavor to deal with this issue was in an address at the Museum of Science and Industry, Chicago, on April 23, 1980. I have benefited from comments by William Kruskal and Robert S. Mullikin, and my debt to John T. Wilson for his help is large.

bel Prizes since 1944. Before World War II, among the prize-winning physicists, chemists, and those in physiology/medicine, only three out of fifty-one were from this country. During the two decades after 1944, half the Nobel Prizes in these categories were awarded to U.S. scientists, and more recently (1975–79) virtually two-thirds have gone to Americans. It is now being said that in the years ahead fewer U.S. scientists will be winning Nobel Prizes, since the sciences in Western Europe and Japan are advancing at a faster rate than in the United States and the creativity of academic scientists in the United States is being reduced by overregulation.

The diminishing returns of Big Science suggest that it may be subject to a long cycle. Such cycles and diminishing returns have a familiar economic ring. But science and economics are not supposed to mix, because economics is too close to the foibles of man. I am aware of the risk of discussing this topic. There is much truth in Frank Knight's famous Law of Talk: "The more intelligent people are, the more certain they are to disagree on matters of social principle and policy, and the more acute will be the disagreement." I also know that economists do not do what needs to be done to make friends. Scientists do not take kindly to the idea of costs and benefits. Governments are wary of being friendly with academic economists. The only real friends that economists have are impersonal, adverse events: inflation, unemployment, and hard times.

Whether the advances in science are made for their own sake or for their practical usefulness, these two achievements are joint products. One always gets both wool and mutton in producing sheep. My approach in evaluating science research rests on two propositions:

1. Advances in science tend to augment the productive capacity of the economy and to improve the welfare of people.[1]

2. The contributions of science have the attributes of *public goods*, which implies that there is not a sufficient

1. See, in this connection, Edward Shils, "Faith, Utility, and the Legitimacy of Science," *Dædalus* 103 (Summer 1974): 1–15.

incentive for business enterprises to invest in that part of science which generates public goods.

Proceeding on these propositions, we face two different issues: the problem of ascertaining the economic value of the public goods that we obtain from advances in science, and the organizational problem in the public sector that provides most of the funds for science research. It is probably true that the value of the contributions of science in general exceeds the normal rates of return on investments, and that academic scientists acquire more personal satisfaction from their work than do scientists in government and in business research establishments, and for that reason accept a somewhat lower salary. The key unsettled issue pertains to the distortions that are a consequence of financing and regulating science research.

In addition to these two propositions and the associated problems, there are several side issues to be pondered. Our large national research laboratories, accelerators, telescopes, ocean observation ships, and instrumentation for control, precision, and computation entail large investments in plant and equipment. What we have are many large, lumpy investments, which are, so it appears, indivisible. Is it possible to tailor modern science research to fit what small countries can do? Compared with that of any other noncommunist country, the size of the science research establishment of the United States corresponds to that of General Motors in its domain. (In expenditures and number of scientists, the Soviet Union and the United States are both very large. But there is a difference: the Soviet Union is more inefficient than we are!) Few low-income countries have the scientific talent and funds to launch and maintain scientific research.

In 1972 there were 129 low-income countries that had under 50 million inhabitants each; 49 of them had populations of fewer than a million people.[2] They were both poor and small. The prospects are also dim that most of the petroleum exporting nations, rich as they are currently, will soon become capable of developing viable science research

2. Based on *World Bank Atlas: Population, Per Capita Product and Growth Rates* (Washington, D.C.: World Bank, 1974).

establishments. Among the large low-income countries, Brazil, India, and Mexico are viable in research, but agricultural research aside, at least four-fifths of the world's countries are not about to do any appreciable amount of basic science research. They simply cannot afford it. General Motors would be a monstrosity in Sri Lanka, or in Tanzania, or in Guatemala. How divisible is modern science research?

We have become enamored of large research institutes and large programs, which are difficult to administer and subject to what is known in economics as diminishing returns to scale. Some of them are wholesalers of research funds allocated under accountability regulations that burden small research enterprises. Creativity in research is, however, predominantly the hallmark of individual scientists whose research enterprises are small. It-is my contention that many research establishments have become too large; they are relatively inefficient compared to the small enterprises that best serve individual scientists. The National Institutes of Health are exceedingly large. In federal budget obligations they received a third of all federal basic research funds in 1979. There are also large research programs in other fields, supported mainly by the National Science Foundation.[3]

What is lost sight of in this overorganization of research is that small basic research enterprises are mainly in universities. (I am mindful of the fact that all of the 1979 U.S. laureates in science are academicians.) In the funding of large research establishments, the concentration of federal funds has been a consequence of governmental decisions, and in this sense it has been the result of the politics of research.

The proposed 1981 budget makes the Department of Defense the fastest growing *buyer* of basic research—up by 12 percent in real dollars,[4] but to become more dependent on defense funds is not consistent with the freedom of inquiry

3. The scale requirements of some programs no doubt call for large research enterprises, e.g., some types of research in astronomy, nuclear research, accelerators, and ocean-going ships and equipment.
4. Eliot Marshall, "Defense," *Science*, February 8, 1980, pp. 619–20.

of academic scientists. Federal funds allocated in this manner will not reduce the distortions in funding basic research.

Promulgation of social reforms by the federal government within U.S. universities, holding research funds as hostage in enforcing these reforms, is more than a side issue. Who determines what science research is to be done and who allocates the research funds to get it done are major issues inherent in the politics of research.

ECONOMICS AND SCIENCE

Basic science influences our cultural and social behavior. Some of it, usually with a considerable lag, alters our technology. As knowledge, science is a special form of capital which is strictly man-made. It is embodied in scientific literature, in developments such as computers and hybrid corn, and in human beings as human capital. Adding to science entails investment, using scarce resources to gain future returns and satisfactions. Inasmuch as it is an investment, albeit in a special form of capital, it has the attributes of an economic activity.

Advances in knowledge are important in augmenting our productive resources and improving the level of living. Agricultural research is a good example. By the early thirties, plant geneticists created hybrid corn, after twenty-three years of research.[5] Other research contributions pertaining to corn followed, and complementary factors were added. By 1979, though 33 million fewer acres were devoted to corn than in the early thirties, total production was three times as large. In addition to the yield effect, *a remarkable substitute for cropland had been developed.* Such an achievement by plant geneticists is indeed a "powerful engine of production."

The economic value of advances in science is grossly ne-

5. Zvi Griliches, "Research Costs and Social Returns: Hybrid Corn and Related Innovations," *Journal of Political Economy* 66 (October 1958): 419–31. Professor Griliches has for some years been devoting a considerable part of his research to the economics of research and development in the United States.

glected, partly because scientists appear to believe that the value of such achievements is self-evident, which it is not. Anyone who is not a scientist who attempts to determine the value of science is deemed an intruder. Scientists are seldom timid in their own domain on this score, and are often proud of being impractical. They are wary of the economics of research and of intruding economists.

The economics of agricultural research has long been high on the agenda at the University of Chicago.[6] Extensions of theory and the acquisition of data require much effort. The first studies at Chicago concentrated on the United States, and then on Mexico. Former students have also taken on agricultural research in India, and, for particular crops, in Argentina and Brazil. The U.S. studies, which began with corn and poultry, were extended to encompass all agricultural research. The findings are strong on the critical economic issue, namely, that the rates of return, taking into account the failures along with the successes, have exceeded the normal rates of return on investment in the economy.

The antiscience movement is not interested in reliable measurements of the overall economic value of science, but it tends to politicize science. From my long involvement in the economics of agricultural research and of the importance of basic research in this connection, I am inclined to believe that the economic and social returns on our overall investment in science research may be relatively high. But I have serious doubts about the efficiency of parts of the science sector. We are, for instance, spending all too much on cancer research, and not enough on other worthwhile basic research opportunities. Diminishing returns indicate that some classes of research are no longer worthwhile.

Taking basic research to be what gets classified as such, about which I am uneasy, the U.S. taxpayer foots most of the bill. For the most recent year for which figures are complete

6. Theodore W. Schultz, "The Economics of Research and Agricultural Productivity," International Agricultural Development Service Occasional Paper (New York, 1979).

(1978),' 69.3 percent of this research was paid for by the federal government, 14.8 percent by industry, 9.9 percent by universities, and 6 percent by various nonprofit institutions. Who actually did this research? The answer is that universities and their affiliates did 59.1 percent of it, federal agencies 16.1 percent, industry 16.1 percent, and nonprofit institutions other than universities 8.7 percent. Since money matters, the federal government has most of the leverage. It presumably has complete say over the 16 percent of this research that is done by federal agencies. For the basic research that is done by industry, industry puts up three dollars for every dollar allocated to it by government. For that done by the various nonprofit institutions other than universities, the government holds a 60 percent share. The universities, who do virtually three-fifths of the basic research, are in the weakest bargaining position. Their money leverage consists of only one dollar of their "own" against four dollars of federal funds. In this sense, they control a minor share of their basic research enterprises. Herein lies the rub.

The economics of who should pay for basic science, and under what conditions, is fairly simple for the small part which is done by industry on its own account, for profit. For the rest, we are in the domain of public goods, which must be paid for by public funds and by private patrons willing to support this public interest. What is treated all too lightly, however, is the fact that decisions have to be made on what research, and how much of each class, is most worthwhile doing, relative to its cost. It is not sufficient to leave all aspects of these decisions to Congress and the executive branch of government. *The need is great for public information on the value of research in negotiating with the electorate for the autonomy of our universities.*

Federal funding of research is not institutionalized to support academic research directly. The Department of Energy is flooded with funds for research which it is incapable of allocating for either applied or basic research. The proposed large increase in the 1981 budget for basic research to be ad-

---

7. *National Patterns of R and D Resources*, NSF–78–313 (Washington, D.C.: National Science Foundation, 1978) p. 4.

ministered by the defense establishment is an indirect, and unsatisfactory, way of funding academic research. Nor is the large indirect funding of this research via the National Aeronautics and Space Administration much better.

There is some comfort in knowing that the distortions of our research are not what they must be in the Soviet Union. The number of scientists with advanced degrees in the physical and life sciences is slightly higher in the Soviet Union. In physics and astronomy the numbers are about the same. We have more in chemistry and in biology. According to Nolting and Feshback, Soviet scientists in agriculture who have advanced degrees outnumber those in U.S. agriculture by at least 70 percent,[8] and Boyce and Evenson show a larger difference.[9] But agricultural science publications "screened for quality" by three international abstracting journals show that the average annual number of publications by Soviet scientists for 1969–73 was 2,690, while for the United States the comparable number was 4,700.[10] In 1929 I spent some time at the then well-known wheat research experiment station at Rostov on the Don. At that time, which was before the collectivization of agriculture, that experiment station was doing work comparable in quality to that in the United States. In 1960, when I was a guest of the All Soviet Academy of Science, it was obvious that the quality of agricultural research had declined substantially. Except in the case of sunflowers, I know of no agricultural productivity advances in the Soviet Union that have come from Soviet research. Agricultural research has been seriously impaired by Soviet doctrine and centralized control.

Our government also has a large measure of monopoly control over basic research, and it is wishful thinking to believe that it will fade away. John T. Wilson began a recent analysis with "Grand Designs: Grand Illusions" and found

---

8. L. E. Nolting and M. Feshback, "R. and D Employment in the U.S.S.R.," *Science*, February 1, 1980, pp. 493–503.

9. James K. Boyce and Robert E. Evenson, *Agricultural Research and Extension Programs* (New York: Agricultural Development Council, 1975).

10. L. E. Nolting and M. Feshback, "R and D Development in the U.S.S.R.," *Science*, February 1, 1980, Table 12, p. 502.

that "whether [or not] one is inclined to view the relationships between the federal government and higher education in broad cyclical terms, as something which is currently just short of disastrous," these relationships have been greatly impaired from what they were during the fifties and sixties.[11] (Wilson's perception and criticism are grounded in his experiences as an NSF administrator and as the recent past president of the University of Chicago.) Gerard Piel's address to the American Philosophical Society a year ago is both cogent and succinct:

> If the autonomy of American universities is to be secured on public support, the necessary protections cannot be decreed by the Executive Branch of the Federal government. Nor can Congress legislate the guarantee. The autonomy of our universities must be negotiated with the electorate. People must be asked to render their support of the university with the full understanding of its mission. . . . Some significant percentage of the regular voters must be ready to entertain such a proposal, for thirty million college graduates are at large in the population.[12]

The public is understandably confused about the value of science. Scientists, except for those in agricultural research, have done all too little to inform the electorate about science and to negotiate for its support. As a part of this negotiation, scientists must face up to the many sources of confusion identified by Philip Handler.[13] Scientists must expose "the anti-scientific and anti-rationalistic" movements, the "faddist approaches to nutrition," and the "unfounded allegations of environmental hazards." Scientists must "unfrock the charlatan" in order to establish the credibility of science with the electorate. They must also "contain the feckless debates concerning the magnitude of the risk of proliferation" from breeder reactors. They must challenge the foolish arguments for a "risk-free society"; if they don't,

11. John T. Wilson, "Higher Education and the Washington Scene: 1980" (University of Chicago, October 1979). Quoted with permission.
12. Gerard Piel, "On Promoting Useful Knowledge," *Proceedings of the American Philosophical Society*, December 28, 1979, pp. 337–40.
13. "The Future of American Science," an address to the Illinois Institute of Technology, Chicago, January 29, 1980.

"we succumb to a national failure of nerve." A telling part of Handler's remarks is that "a decade ago it may have been desirable to flag public attention to potential hazards. . . . But that can also set us off in the wrong direction. . . . And it has done so at the expense of resources and talent that might more usefully have been utilized" in more important scientific endeavors.

My plea is that we dispel this confusion and find ways to negotiate with the electorate for financial support that is allocated directly to scientists with a minimum of accountability regulations. The autonomy of our universities is currently being impaired. Academic scientists are too beholden to government. The harsh truth is we have been moving bit by bit closer to the Soviet model. Unless this tendency is reversed, in time fewer U.S. scientists will be making the annual pilgrimage to Alfred Nobel's Mecca.

DISTORTIONS OF ECONOMIC RESEARCH

Although the sciences are harassed by antiscience movements, their legitimacy and utility is more firmly established than that of economics. Governments are wary of economists who are not beholden to them. Churchill referred to Arthur Pigou as "that great economist" when he cited him in support of his policy. But when Pigou expressed disagreement, Churchill called him a sheltered academic. The reports of the National Academy of Sciences are defended before congressional committees by the academy. There is no equivalent defense for the work of economists. More important, academic research in economics is in its infancy compared to research in the sciences, and the funding of research tends to distort economic research much more than it does scientific research.[14]

14. I began to deal with this issue in a paper given at the Fiftieth Anniversary Celebration of the Social Sciences Research Building, University of Chicago, on December 16, 1979, which benefited from the comments of D. Gale Johnson and William H. Kruskal. As I extended the original treatment, I became indebted to Zvi Griliches and T. Paul Schultz for their critical comments.

Economists have prospered from a long boom in the demand for their services, largely a consequence of the activities of a new breed of research institution. These institutions are in the ascendancy in competing for research funds, and in this competition the comparative advantage of university research is declining. While foundations are contributing to this new pattern in economic research, federal research funds are vastly more important in financing it. Booms tend to produce distortions, and patrons are not renowned for their neutrality when it comes to economic research. "Targeted research" and "mission-oriented research" objectives have become enshrined in most projects that are funded by governmental agencies, and also in some foundation grants. Nor are private patrons innocent in this respect.

I do not want to imply that all economic research prior to two or three decades ago was being done by universities. Large businesses, banks, and trade associations have long employed economists to do research deemed to be useful to them. Organized labor and national farm organizations have done likewise, especially since the New Deal era. There are also bureaus of long standing, staffed with competent economists, in the federal departments of agriculture, commerce, labor, and the treasury, which have been, and continue to be, engaged in the measurement of economic components and in producing economic statistics. Among the early not-for-profit pioneers, two are noteworthy. The National Bureau of Economic Research, which was guided at the outset by the distinguished economist Wesley Mitchell, did yeoman work. The NBER sought the assistance and criticism of university economists. It engaged in measurement and in producing data that required facilities and staff that no university could afford. The remarkable research of Simon Kuznets and his associates for the NBER developed the concepts and the measurements that are required in national income accounting. Currently, however, the research of the NBER is less concerned with improving the quality of economic data and sustained data gathering and more concerned with current policy issues. It has also become substantially dependent on public funds. The Brookings Institution, which is the other major, long-established research organization, has been much favored by foundation grants and also by public funds. During its early years under the leadership of Henry Moulton, and at times since then, a good deal of the economic research of Brookings has been closely identified with that of particular current policy objectives. Other research entities that are less well known include the National Planning Association, which dates back to the New Deal period, and has been and continues to be strongly policy-oriented; and the Committee for Economic Development, set up following World War II to protest the dominant views of business organizations, which contributed substantially in clarifying some of the then policy issues.

Each of the twelve long-established Federal Reserve Banks has a research department headed by a vice-president. The economics staff in the system's Washington headquarters is large. Most of the research of the Federal Reserve system is, however, confined to in-house purposes, and all too few of the studies are published in professional journals. For a few years, while C. O. Hardy was there, the Kansas City bank was an exception, as the St. Louis bank has been more recently.

During the past twenty-five years the proliferation of institutes engaged in economic research has been extraordinary. They have emerged, as already noted, in response to large increases in the funds available for specific economic policy research. A drastic shift has occurred in the allocation of research funds in favor of those that specialize in such research and are not encumbered by being too closely connected with a university. Some on-campus institutes that are not hampered by the academic duties of departments of economics have been favored. In large measure, this shift has come about because most university departments of economics are deemed to be too rigid, because they resist interdisciplinary and team research projects, and because they are too committed to traditional Ph.D. research, to theoretical studies, and to esoteric empirical work. Moreover, universities are in large measure viewed as being either un-able or unwilling to shape up and do the type of policy re-search that is wanted.

The list of nonprofit research institutes is long: over 300 in economic research alone.[15] There are institutes that spe-cialize in economic development, econometric models, in-ternational trade, taxation, enterprise, education, urban development, energy, manpower, consumer affairs, envi-ronmental reforms, legal issues, health, population, and poverty. Nor are the research funds for these purposes small; for example, the federal government is allocating approx-imately $90 million a year to support poverty research.[16] Since the growth of this industry has occurred predomi-nantly outside of the confines of the universities, the im-plication is that university economic research has not satis-fied this specialized demand.

Clearly some private patrons of economic research, foun-dations, and virtually all governmental agencies have de-cided that universities lack the capacity or the desire to do the research that they demand. One alternative option that has been pursued by some foundations is to undertake and manage a good deal of the research they want as an in-house activity. This is a way of establishing new policy areas, which then serve to determine the type of grant proposals that will be considered. In a variant of this, the Carnegie Foundation established the Carnegie Commission on High-er Education and allocated some millions of dollars to it. The Ford Foundation's first in-house report on energy, *A Time to Choose* (1974), is an example of harmful economic policy advocacy, befitting a populist approach in coping with the energy problem. The third Ford Foundation in-house en-ergy report, *Energy: The Next Twenty Years*, prepared under

15. Archie M. Palmer, ed., *Research Centers Directory* (Detroit: Gale Research Company, 1979), 6th ed., lists 304 nonprofit research organiza-tions in the United States and Canada engaged in economic research. A good number of them have some sort of affiliation with a university.

16. National Research Council, National Academy of Sciences, *Evaluat-ing Federal Support of Poverty Research* (G. K. Hall, 1979; rpt. Cambridge, Mass.: Schenkman, 1979).

the direction of Hans H. Landsberg, makes good economic sense.

A few of the new research institutes are doing first-rate research and producing analytical studies of high quality. A notable example is the performance over the past twenty-five years of Resources for the Future, a relatively small institute that concentrates on studies pertaining to natural resources. Although natural resources are a highly sensitive political area, RFF has not become dependent on government project funds, and has successfully resisted efforts to bring about a "forced marriage" with another, much larger institution that has the proper policy qualifications.

The Office of Naval Analysis and Air Force Project RAND supported significant work in mathematical and theoretical economics during the 1950s and 1960s. Ph.D. and postdoctoral research in human capital was broadly supported by the National Institute of Mental Health during the 1970s, until it was abruptly terminated because it was then deemed to be insufficiently applied, given the legal mandate of NIMH. Earlier research in agricultural economics at Chicago and Harvard, supported by USDA funds, was also terminated abruptly, in this case because of the whims of the chairman of a congressional appropriation committee. The majority in Congress tend to be opposed to having governmental agencies allocate research funds to economists who are presumed to be critical of particular public programs.

No doubt a good deal of the research financed by federal funds and done by institutes which are not affiliated with a university serves the purpose of the granting agency. But the success of some of these new institutes does not resolve the question of whether or not academic economic thought and research are useful in determining the merits and limitations of economic policies. The professional personnel who manage the governmental agencies that allocate funds under the restrictions imposed by Congress are constrained, and thus not free, leaving aside the issue of the required competence, to determine the type of university support that would best serve the function of academic economists. The National Science Foundation may be viewed as an exception, but all too few NSF grants support criticism of the state of economic analysis. Despite political opposition to economics, NSF has supported the research of Nelson and Winter criticizing the profit-maximizing analysis of the behavior of firms, Fogel's attack on society's institutions, and Lucas's criticism of existing macro-orthodoxy. The distortions about which we should be concerned also entail the accommodations made by universities to obtain research funds from foundations, from government, and from the new breed of institutes when they offer to subcontract some of their ongoing research. Of the federal basic research budget that supports social science research, about 60 percent was channeled to universities in 1973, but by 1978 the proportion had decreased to 47 percent. The adverse cumulative effect on academic economists is dramatic.[17]

Tensions between what economists do and what the dominant institutions of society want them to do antedate the current period by centuries. The differences on basic economic issues were as pervasive in the past as the tensions associated with the recent developments on which I have dwelt. Historically economists have, inter alia, criticized the economic doctrines of the church, the state, the property-owning class (landlords), and the mercantile doctrine. The nature of the critique changes over time. The scholarly studies of Jacob Viner, for example, feature the economic doctrines of the early Christian fathers, of the scholastics, of the secularizing tendencies in Catholic social thought, and of Protestantism in relation to the rise of capitalism.[18] The doctrines of the church pertaining to usury, to the sterility of money capital, and to the just price are examined in the context of the then prevailing scholarship. There is also a

17. Richard C. Atkinson, "Federal Support in the Social Sciences," *Science*, February 22, 1980, p. 829; an editorial comment based on his remarks at the Fiftieth Anniversary Celebration of the Social Sciences Research Building, University of Chicago, on December 16, 1979.

18. Jacob Viner, *Religious Thought and Economic Society*, four chapters of an unfinished work, ed. Jacques Melitz and Donald Winch (Durham, N.C.: Duke University Press, 1978).

critical essay by Viner on providence in the social order.[19] While the tensions between religious and economic thought have declined, some differences persist on particular social and economic issues inherent in the doctrines with respect to the relationship between church and state.

The remarkable decline in rent from land relative to the earnings of labor and other sources of income in the high-income countries has very much reduced the social and political influence of landlords, and the tensions between them and economic thought have diminished as a consequence. Meanwhile, however, some of the economic entitlements demanded by businesses, organized labor, organized agricultural groups, and environmental groups strain the relationship between them and economics.

We are in an era in which the tensions between the university and the state have become increasingly acute. These difficulties are not restricted to private universities, nor are they specific to the United States. They are worldwide, although they differ greatly among the more than 150 nation-states. In most countries, the intellectual independence of universities is seriously constrained, especially so in the case of social and economic thought and research. What these nation-states want makes the relationship fragile and subjects it to much uncertainty for universities. Even in the United States, the more heavily dependent the university is on the patronage of government, the less the freedom of inquiry in the social sciences.

Throughout much of the world, academic economists are decidedly beholden to governments. It is obviously so in the Soviet Union, China, and in other countries that have centralized control of their economies. Many low-income countries have opted for a partially controlled economy and for external subsidies to equalize the differences in per capita income between them and the rich countries. Governments presume that academic economists can, when required, ra-

19. Jacob Viner, *The Role of Providence in the Social Order: An Essay in Intellectual History* (Philadelphia: American Philosophical Society, 1972; paperback ed., Princeton, N.J.: Princeton University Press, 1976).

tionalize these objectives. Even in Western Europe and North America, where democratic governments have long prevailed, tensions have increased during recent decades on issues pertaining to economic policy.

It stands repeating that within the university, economics is more vulnerable to off-campus intrusions than university research in the natural sciences. The vulnerability of biological research to governmental regulation has, however, become serious, but even at that economics is decidedly more exposed to subversion. Then, too, recent antiscience movements are changing the relationship between science and the public perception of the sciences, and in this process these movements have to some extent politicized the allocation of public funds for science research. Edward Shils has dealt thoughtfully with this issue in his essay, "Faith, Utility and the Legitimacy of Science." Would that there were a comparable essay on the utility of economics.

A CRITIQUE OF ACADEMIC ECONOMICS

Despite inflation and the financial stringency faced by universities, academic economists have not fared badly, in large part because of the nonuniversity market for their services. By this market test, it would be all too easy to conclude that economists are highly productive. But, in fact, the utility that either the university or society derives from what academic economists do is not obvious. While economists are not reluctant to ascertain the value derived from the use of scarce resources by people in any other activity, they are shy when it comes to reckoning the utility of their own work. Most academic economists are complacent about their freedom of inquiry, about safeguarding their university functions, and about the conditions under which research funds are made available to them by institutions other than the university. This complacency about the usefulness of inquiry that is free from outside intrusion is exemplified in their failure publicly to challenge private patrons, foundations, and governmental agencies on their allocation of funds for economic research. But to do this competently requires firm knowledge of the utility of economic thought and the research appropriate to the functions of the university. It also requires courage, because it entails the risk of alienating the patrons and causing them to reduce further their support of university research. This risk is neatly avoided by the art of accommodation—by quietly and gracefully submitting proposals for research grants that seem to fit the demands of the patrons.

The distinction between the concepts of applied and basic research is not meaningful in determining the function of academic economics. The now fashionable concepts of targeted and mission-oriented research are, as a rule, subterfuges for intrusion. Peer review of economic research proposals by individuals who are selected by the granting agency, notably so in the case of some governmental agencies, is a convenient device for obtaining sufficient differences in evaluations to give the administrator of the agency a free hand in deciding whether or not to approve the proposal.

The forte of academic economics is comprehensive analysis and criticism of private economic behavior and public economic policies. Comprehensiveness in this context does not restrict academic economics to improvements in the internal consistency of economic logic, quantitative analytical tools, and empirical analysis, although these endeavors are exceedingly important. Academic economists cannot divorce themselves from society and from the insights of the humanities and of history. Hayek could say with good grace, "Nobody can be a great economist who is only an economist," and added that "an economist who is only an economist is likely to become a nuisance if not a positive danger." [20] The "dilemma of specialization" remains unresolved.

Scholarly criticism of society's institutions by economists is at a low ebb—criticism, for example, of the quality of the work of Jacob Viner, Frank Knight, Oscar Lange, and Harry Johnson, and also of Thorstein Veblen. Their studies and publications were not shaped by governmental agencies,

20. F. A. Hayek, "The Dilemma of Specialization," in *The State of the Social Sciences* (Chicago: University of Chicago Press, 1956).

foundations, or by private patrons. It is unlikely that university economists of their caliber and with their scholarly interests could obtain funds for research from off-campus sources. What is also distressing is that the search for talent is for a different set of economic qualifications, and as a consequence there is a lack of incentives for the coming generation of economists to acquire the competence that is required to pursue scholarly criticism of economic doctrines and of society's institutions. One of the primary functions of at least a subset of economists is to devote their talents to comprehensive social and economic criticism, with freedom of inquiry protected by their university.

The criticism that is lacking is fairly obvious. There are all too few competent critical studies of the economics of the host of United Nations organizations, despite the fact that most of them are debasing economics. Whereas the early economic doctrines of the Church were supported, as Viner has shown, by considerable scholarship, the economic doctrines that prevail within the United Nations are not similarly burdened. It is to the lasting credit of Harry Johnson that he challenged not only these but also other institutions of society.[21] Peter Bauer, in his dissent on economic development doctrines, is another exception.[22] The pronounced drift toward soft economics on the part of some foundations—in large measure a consequence of a "live-and-let-live" policy which requires accommodation to the demands of the prevailing international organizations and to the current politicized demands within the United States—goes unchallenged by economists.

In analyzing choices and scarcities, economists tend to hold fast to the preferences of individuals and families, including the preferences served by household activities. Some of society's institutions, however, distort these preferences. There is a pervasive intellectual and popular commitment to the belief that the failures of the market are the

21. Harry G. Johnson, *On Economics and Society* (Chicago: University of Chicago Press, 1975).
22. P. T. Bauer, *Dissent on Development* (Cambridge, Mass.: Harvard University Press, 1972). Studies and Debates in Development Economics.

primary flaw in the economy. Each interest group has its own agenda of such market failures. To overcome them, an increasing number of organized groups seek protection and redress by means of public programs and institutions created by government. Business groups have a long history of serving their special interests by this means, and organized labor and commodity groups have been doing so for decades. This pluralistic process is currently compounded by the politics of health, of the aged, of poverty, of income transfers, of energy, of environmental politics, and others. The resulting modifications of the political economy in general do not correct actual market failures, but tend to bring about other forms of economic failure. In part by design, but mainly unwittingly, some of the specialized research in departments of economics supports this special-interest fragmentation of the economy by governmental intervention, which is surely not the function of academic economists.

Economic research in most universities is less than optimum for several additional reasons. Ph.D. research in general is not well organized. There is a lack of opportunities for graduate students to make progress reports on their research at regularly scheduled meetings organized to provide useful criticism by other graduate students and faculty. Members of the faculty in charge of supervising Ph.D. research are frequently involved in off-campus consulting to private business and government agencies, diverting their intellectual endeavors from the research that is appropriate to the functions of the universities.[23] Although the administration and faculty of universities proclaim that research is one of their major and vital functions, the bureaucratic financial

23. I am uneasy about some aspects of this, but the evidence reported by Carl V. Patton and James D. Marver suggests that from 1969 to 1975 there has not been any increase in academic consulting. The evidence also indicates, controlling for type of institution and rank of faculty, that paid consultants do somewhat more research, more graduate instruction, publish more, and more of them serve as chairmen of departments than do faculty who are not paid consultants. See Patton and Marver, "Paid Consulting by American Academics," *Educational Record* 60 (Spring 1979): 175–84; and their earlier paper, "The Correlates of Consultation: American Academics in the 'Real World,'" *Higher Education* 5 (August 1976): 319–35.

organization of the university provides little direct support for economic research. This financial issue is more acute in economics than in the sciences, though economics does not require laboratories and expensive physical facilities. All an empirical economist needs is a research assistant, perhaps a programmer, access to a suitable computer, and funds to acquire data.

The charters of our not-for-profit foundations do not require that they primarily support short-range politicized economic policy research. Foundations have on occasion provided funds for comprehensive, long-range policy research. The Rockefeller Foundation, for example, has generously funded the agricultural economics workshop at the University of Chicago continuously since the early forties. At an earlier period, the Rockefeller Foundation on its own initiative offered the Ames group of economists a generous grant, without any restrictions on the range of policy issues that would be investigated. I would be less than grateful if I did not acknowledge the six recent years of support I have received from the Ford Foundation for research and writing of my own choosing, and there are, of course, other examples of this type of support by foundations. The secular drift has, however, been to support the wide array of new institutes that specialize in current, short-range economic policy issues.

Government agencies do not, however, have the freedom that foundations have when it comes to providing funds for comprehensive economic policy research. Such agencies are constrained by congressional mandates that determine the research purposes to which federal funds can be put. The National Science Foundation has more degrees of freedom than other government agencies, but it, too, is hampered by short-range tests of useful research imposed by Congress. Congress has wantonly politicized the policy research of the vast number of administrative units of government that have been established to promulgate declared policies. The politics of research is bad for economic research. Whereas the funds authorized by Congress for research are large, in allocating these funds virtually every administrative agency of government is restricted to research that will support its particular policy mandate. It is not within the domain of the agency to finance competent economic criticism of its own activities or of the adverse effects of economic policy fragmentation.

Federal research funds have not always been allocated in this perverse manner. The Purnell Act is a clear case of federal funding of university research that has continuity and stability, sufficiently so to make tenured appointments. Fifty years ago the Purnell Act authorized an annual appropriation of $60,000 ($250,000 in 1979 prices) for each of the land-grant universities, to be used for rural social science research.[24] Agricultural economics is the primary recipient of these federal funds, which provide continuing core support for faculty and Ph.D. research. This research is not beholden to the federal government, although it has not always been free of political intrusions on the part of the states.

The thrust of my argument is that one of the primary functions of academic economists is to question society's institutions. Economists are all too complacent about their freedom of inquiry. They are not sufficiently vigilant in safeguarding their function as educators. They should give a high priority to scholarly criticism of the economics of society's institutions. The distortions of economic research will not fade away by accommodating the patrons of research funds.

24. Theodore W. Schultz with the assistance of Lawrence W. Witt, *Training and Recruiting of Personnel in the Rural Social Sciences* (Washington, D.C.: American Council on Education, 1941).

7
Distortions by the International Donor Community

Since World War II, a new institution has developed, which I shall refer to as the International Donor Community. Its purpose, broadly defined, is foreign aid. In common with other political-economic institutions, it influences what people in many countries do privately and what their governments do in their policies. What are its economic effects? Does it favor more or less government intervention in production and consumption, in internal and external trade, and in the distribution of personal income? Does it have the classical attributes of liberalism or of mercantilism? I shall not deal directly with these unsettled issues. To do so would require a consideration of the supporting ideas and underlying philosophical and normative issues, a task beyond the scope of this essay.[1] I shall concentrate instead on various aspects of foreign aid and trade on which I have, over the years, done a bit of work.

The picture of policies affecting economic activities since

My initial approach to this issue was presented to the faculties in economics, University of California, Berkeley; I subsequently extended the analysis in a paper invited by the American Agricultural Economics Association meetings, Urbana-Champaign, Illinois, July 29, 1980. I draw upon these presentations in this chapter, and am indebted to John M. Letiche for his helpful suggestions.

1. These issues are considered briefly in the early part of my lecture, "The Economic Value of Human Time Over Time," in *Lectures in Agricultural Economics*, bicentennial year lectures sponsored by the USDA Economic Research Service (Washington, D.C.: USDA, 1977).

World War II is blurred by inconsistencies. The extraordinary recovery of Japan and West Germany was made possible in considerable part by their opportunities to trade.
Many low-income countries also benefited substantially
from freer international trade and from the general economic stability and economic growth of the major indus-
trialized countries. Taiwan, Hong Kong, and Singapore are
outstanding examples. But there has been a pervasive tendency to politicize economic activities. Although early classical economics prevailed over the then established doctrine
of mercantilism, there now is a much more comprehensive
doctrine in support of government intervention in all manner of economic activities. I shall contend that many international donor agencies have an antimarket bias and a
propensity to support government intervention at the expense of economic productivity. Donor agencies are strong
for social reforms, but they are weak when it comes to
productivity.

I now return to the economics of being poor and the difficulties we have in comprehending the preferences and resource constraints that determine the choices which people
in low-income countries make. These difficulties are pervasive in the foreign aid. My purpose is to explore the economic effects of foreign aid, as administered by donor agencies, on farm people in low-income countries. My economic
critique is restricted to agricultural research, capital for agricultural development, dumping of commodities, tying of
foreign aid to donor goods and services, arrangements for
foreign experts, and the equity-productivity tension created
by donor agencies. I shall touch on the neglect of the functions of the market and the distortions of agricultural
incentives.

The United States has long been a donor of various forms
of aid, but the economics of aid is beset by puzzles. Why was
the aid provided by the Marshall Plan successful although it
was available for only a few years? Compared to it, why has
the large amount of aid to low-income countries since
World War II been much less successful? Why did the Point

Four Latin American Aid program contribute so little to the productivity of agriculture? Why have private foundations and a large number of international donor agencies, except in the case of agricultural research, had very limited success in improving the economic environment and the schooling of farm people in low-income countries?

The International Donor Community is large and complex. I can do no more than explore what it does and what effects it has on farm people. It should be noted at the outset that most of the members of this community have evolved a "live-and-let-live" policy in support of their common interest, which is less dependent on the support of the countries that receive aid than it is on maintaining and increasing the financial support they obtain from the high-income and oil-rich countries. There are many donor agencies, engaged in an array of aid activities. A good number of them maintain regional and country offices. They recruit and finance development and welfare experts, donate resources in kind (mainly food and agricultural commodities), provide emergency relief, finance agricultural research and extension work, control large funds for agricultural development, and acquire stocks of food grains, presumably to stabilize the supply available to low-income countries. The International Donor Community supports the World Bank and various regional banks. Donor agencies also produce and distribute information tailored to their objectives. I shall refer to all these various activities as foreign aid.

Foreign aid is still an ambiguous concept in economics; the dialogue between economic theory and observable foreign aid is not one of the cogent parts of economics. My presentation is exploratory because there is *no generally accepted economic rationale for foreign aid* on which I can build to determine its economic effects with any precision. Studies of foreign aid that are based on political considerations are not, as a rule, useful when it comes to economic analysis.

The resources that enter into foreign aid are sufficiently large to have economic effects not only on the countries that make these resources available but also on the countries that receive and use them. Rather than consider the re-source issues that impinge on the donor countries, I intend to examine the organizational process of distributing foreign aid, and search for the reasons for its economic successes and failures.

While I was with the army of occupation in Europe I had the good luck to anticipate the reasons for the success of the Marshall Plan. The war had destroyed a great deal of physical capital, whereas human capital had been much less impaired. Recovery depended primarily on rebuilding factories and houses, and acquiring equipment and inventories. The Marshall Plan contributed a good deal of capital for these purposes. Western Europe and Japan, given strong market demands and international trade, recovered rapidly. This is explained when account is taken of the economic importance of human capital and of domestic and international markets. But, as stated earlier, this lesson, so evident from the Marshall Plan experience, has been persistently over-looked in providing aid to low-income countries. All too lit-tle foreign aid has been allocated to enhance the stock of human capital and to strengthen markets in these countries.

The puzzle of the agricultural failure of Point Four aid is also instructive. In the early fifties, the Ford Foundation made a generous grant to the National Planning Association to evaluate the technical assistance of Point Four through-out Latin America. I agreed to serve as the director of that enterprise and was helped by highly competent colleagues. Investigating the reasons for the failure of the agricultural part of the program, we discovered that the design of Point Four was based on the assumption that the available, un-used results from agricultural research called for extension activities. Extension services were developed cooperatively with the host governments. But they soon faded away be-cause there was little worthwhile technical information for them to distribute to farmers.

I have long been concerned about the differences among the major foundations in their approaches to agriculture. The results are a record of pluses and minuses. The early Ford Foundation agricultural program in India was a premature commitment to extension activity, and the Kellogg Foundation is unfortunately committed by its charter to extension activities. By contrast, the agricultural research program launched by the Rockefeller Foundation in cooperation with the government of Mexico was a highly successful innovation. The International Agricultural Research Centers are a major innovation in principle on a par with the work of the Rockefeller Foundation in Mexico. The first centers were financed by the Ford and Rockefeller Foundations, joined by the Canadian International Research Development Centre, which in the early years operated as one would expect a private foundation to function. The total annual budget of the twelve International Agricultural Research Centers has come to exceed $100 million. Most of the funds now come from the World Bank and regional banks, from Canadian aid, from Western European donors, from Japan, and from the U.S. Agency for International Development (A.I.D.)[2]

Farm people in low-income countries have virtually no direct contact with the international donor agencies, except in the case of agricultural research. And this, too, is very limited. For all practical purposes farm people have no influence on what these donor agencies are doing that affects their well-being. Foreign aid is predominantly a public activity. Governments and UN agencies, which are also public entities, deal with governments. Most of the reckoning of the economic effects on farm people is swamped by political considerations. In view of the heterogeneity among low-income countries—including their governments—and given the various classes of foreign aid, there are few useful generalizations.

Foreign aid to support agricultural production research has been fairly successful, but it has neglected farm house-

2. For a brief treatment of the organizational issues that characterize these centers, see my "The Economics of Research and Agricultural Productivity," *International Agricultural Development Service Occasional Paper* (New York, 1979).

hold production research. Nor has it supported meaningful research in low-income countries to determine the nutrition of farm and nonfarm people.

The growth in agricultural research oriented to the requirements of low-income countries is a major achievement, much of which has occurred since World War II. It has an international dimension. Although the International Donor Community has, in general, a spotty record in its economic effects on agriculture in low-income countries, the notable exception is its contribution to the development of agricultural research. Agricultural research centers are a large part of that contribution. But, these international agricultural research centers, good as they are, are not a substitute for ongoing national agricultural research.

Some foreign aid for agricultural research has been unsuccessful. Point Four, as already noted, failed on this score. U.S. bilateral aid has a mixed record, most of which is marred by a lack of continuity in its support of.agricultural research. Congress is largely to blame. It has imposed on the aid agency an organization that is inefficient in providing funds to help build national agricultural research experiment stations and laboratories in low-income countries. A.I.D. does not have the professional staff to do this; nor does it have an appropriate mandate to finance such research on a long-term basis. I would not advise any low-income country to depend upon such foreign aid for resources in developing its agricultural research capacity.

Agricultural research is largely organized to improve the biological possibilities of crops and livestock. Its genetic and breeding success is not in doubt. Too little attention is, however, given to the economic constraints that farmers in low-income countries face. Some of the international agricultural research centers are beginning to examine the economics of farmers' responses in adopting new crop varieties. But, the economists on the staffs of these centers have, as yet, a tenuous intellectual footing in their activities.

There is much unevenness among low-income countries in the opportunities that farmers have to take advantage of the contributions of agricultural research, primarily because of the distortions of incentives that they are up against. No donor agency, few host governments, and few agricultural research organizations appear to be aware of the adverse effects of these distortions on the modernization of agriculture. Or, if they are, they act as though they were unconcerned.

Compared to the progress in agricultural research, organized research supported by aid funds to improve the production possibilities of farm households is sadly neglected. Although there is a growing concern, which is long overdue, to improve the opportunities of women in low-income countries, virtually no attention is being given to farm household production, which is in the domain of women. Simple things are called for. For instance, in rural Senegal, grain sorghum, a major food crop, is hard to free from its husk. I recently saw women there using heavy wooden clubs to break this husk—arduous work under the tropical sun. In each of three villages, these women asked me the same question: "Why can't we have a simple hand mill to do this task?" What is called for is research and business enterprise that would make it possible to modernize household production.[3]

There is also a neglect of nutrition research. I know of no international donor agency that has established, in cooperation with a host government, a viable and competent nutrition research center. Instead of supporting such research, donor agencies specialize in making pronouncements on the dire consequences of malnutrition. These pronouncements are largely self-serving. It is not being cynical to infer that the donor agencies know full well that pictures of malnourished children, along with statements on the vast extent of malnutrition, which are as a rule not creditable, serve their self-interest in appealing for more funds. Most of the estimates of the proportion of the population that is malnourished are based on a *fixed calorie* standard. C. H.

3. The International Development Research Center, Canada, has supported some research and enterprises in this area.

Shah[4] provides strong evidence that the tastes or preferences of people play a significant role in determining their
expenditures per calorie of food. In view of Shah's study, estimates of malnutrition based on fixed calorie standards
must be interpreted with great caution. P. V. Sukhatme, who
has devoted much of his career to the study of nutrition,
finds that there are large variations in the energy (calories)
required among individuals, and for the same individual
from day to day and thus overtime.[5]

The modernization of agriculture requires many new
forms of capital. The donor agencies contribute to the supply. Even under the best of circumstances, it is difficult
to allocate capital efficiently in dealings between governments. The test is in the results that are achieved. How
much is this capital contributing to agricultural production?
What is the net yield that is derived from it? Why is it that
no donor agency presents estimates of the private and social
rates of return that are achieved on the capital that it has
allocated? Surely it should do so when the agency makes its
case for more funds. There is no lack of economists in these
agencies who are competent to make these estimates. Since
I do not have access to such estimates, I obviously cannot
establish the economic value of these investments.

Foreign aid to support research aside, my first assessment
turns on the allocation of funds between physical and human capital in promoting agricultural development. In my
judgment, if half of the donor funds that are being allocated
to increase the stock of physical capital in agriculture were
allocated to enhance the abilities of rural people, it would
increase the rate of agricultural development over the next

4. C. H. Shah, "Food Preferences and Nutrition: A Perspective on Poverty in Less Developed Countries," *Indian Journal of Agricultural Economics* 35 (January–March 1980): 1–39.
5. P. V. Sukhatme, "Malnutrition and Poverty," Ninth Lal Bahadur
Shastri Memorial Lecture, Indian Agricultural Research Institute, New
Delhi, January 29, 1977. For a fuller interpretation of the work of Sukhatme
and C. H. Shah, see D. Gale Johnson, "The World Food Situation: Developments During the 1970s and Prospects for the 1980s," University of Chicago
Agricultural Economics Research Paper No. 80–10 (March 1980).

couple of decades substantially compared to the prospects under the prevailing allocation of this capital. In terms of expected returns that are measurable in production activities as modernization proceeds, and the expected personal satisfactions that people derive from their human capital, there is a gross underinvestment in the quality of the population that people want to acquire. While there are many pronouncements by those who administer foreign aid to that effect, little is being done to provide resources for this purpose. The recent World Bank report, *Education and Income*, has real merit.

My next endeavor is to consider some of the well-known increases in agricultural production in low-income countries and ask what has been the contribution of the capital provided by the International Donor Community? Here I have in mind all forms of physical capital: land improvement, irrigation, fertilizer, farm equipment, storage facilities, rural roads, and still other related forms of capital.

On this issue, one needs to ponder the notable successes in agriculture where little or no donor agency capital was involved. The dramatic increase in wheat production in India, entailing many new forms of physical capital, is a case in point. Others include the success in producing palm fruit in Malaysia; in producing soybeans in Brazil, and now also in the Argentine; the recent increases in the production of fresh fruit, wine, and cut flowers in Chile; and the long-standing success in producing fresh vegetables and some fruits in Mexico for the U.S. winter market. The success of Kenya in adopting hybrid corn, using fertilizer, and suppressing pests and insects in growing this corn, is still another example; that country's success in producing tea, coffee, and now also pineapples, likewise belongs on this list. The implication is that where the production possibilities have become favorable via agricultural research, and where price incentives make it worthwhile, most, if not all, of the additional capital is forthcoming from the profitability of the ongoing production. This implication is as valid for small farms as it is for farms which are not so small.

With projects financed by donor agency capital, the production effects have in many cases been zero. Throughout most of central Africa, most capital projects have been failures. Tanzania is an obvious case in point. Going back to the 1960s, the outside capital committed to increase palm-fruit production in Nigeria failed. The field staff economists of the agency that provided the capital analyzed the economic prospects correctly, given the large export tax on palm-fruit products. The project was nevertheless approved and financed.

Where governments are weak, where there is continuing political instability, and where there are all too few trained, experienced, and competent individuals to manage the formation of agricultural capital, capital projects, as they are presently promoted by the World Bank and other agencies, cannot succeed.

There are, of course, a good number of countries that can manage capital projects. They tend to know their capital requirements, and they also insist that projects be tailored accordingly.

Overall, I have the uneasy feeling that, in general, the realized rates of return on these capital projects are below the normal returns on investment in many low-income countries. This assessment does not imply that there are no increases in the capacity of agriculture. What is implied is that the yields are too low.

The malallocation of capital is a pervasive problem. It is, in large measure, a consequence of the prevailing distortions in agricultural product and input prices in many low-income countries. The allocations are also distorted by the funding of massive irrigation projects, which are as a rule a mistake. The Inter-American Development Bank this past year attained its goal of loans for rural development. But it achieved this goal by approving three large irrigation projects toward the end of the year—which in all probability will have extremely low, if not negative, net yields. The allocation and use to which such funds are put are also seriously marred by the prevailing equity doctrines of the International Donor Community.

Aid in kind has the effect of dumping. It is a convenient

way for a donor country to dispose of its own burdensome surpluses, and has the effect of increasing the capacity of the government that receives such aid to continue discriminating against its own agriculture, whether it be by procurement of food grains from farmers below market prices, by marketing boards, or by other means of maintaining a cheap food policy that distorts agricultural incentives. The adverse effect on farmers in India of the vast quantities of P.L. 480 agricultural commodities during the fifties and sixties is a case in point. Our rhetoric was "Food for Peace." Currently, the large amounts of P.L. 480–type aid going to Egypt have the effect of underwriting the bad internal agricultural policies of that government. This form of dumping also impairs the international markets of agricultural commodities.

The extent and effects of tied aid are difficult to observe. Such aid occurs mainly when a donor government insists that a part of the funds and grants made available through bilateral aid be used to purchase its materials, commodities, or services. Although an accounting of tied aid rarely surfaces in published records, there is evidence that over 70 percent of U.S. aid is tied. Privately, economists in low-income countries reveal the consequences of particular tied aid. For example, Sweden recently offered India a generous training grant in forestry. After two years of negotiations, however, the Indian government was unable to eliminate the tied conditions that Sweden insisted upon, and the grant was for that reason not accepted. Weaker countries do not do what India did.

Experts recruited from high-income countries are very expensive. Total costs per expert made available by U.S. aid agencies are about $100,000 a year. In the case of a good number of low-income countries, these donor experts are less qualified than the indigenous corps of experts with whom they work. In view of the high cost and the lack of sufficient qualifications of many experts that are recruited by aid agencies, the waste of aid funds is large. Some of the agricultural personnel that land grant universities designate to serve low-income countries are subject to the same limitations.

At present it is the policy of most members of the International Donor Community to reduce the inequality in the distribution of personal income and wealth, even though it impairs the potential productivity of agriculture. The equity objectives are those that the high-income donor governments find appropriate for their own countries. The higher the personal income of the donor country the less appropriate this approach to the equity problems in low-income countries is. Sweden qualifies as the most serious offender in promoting her concept of equity in providing foreign aid. The effects of her aid in supporting undemocratic governments and in impairing agricultural productivity are lost sight of. These are the consequences, as I see them, in Tanzania. To a lesser degree, other foreign-aid donors are also bent on such equity objectives, at the expense of the potential increases in agricultural productivity to enhance the food supply that agricultural research and high-yielding agricultural investments would make possible. UN aid agencies have the same bias, as does the U.S. Agency for International Development. Congress, in effect, demands such equity objectives, despite the fact that the results of similar domestic policies have failed. Congress has authorized large appropriations to improve the economic lot of small farmers in the United States, and, despite the high level of competence of the personnel that have administered these programs, the results have been failures. Yet Congress expects low-income countries to succeed in undertaking such agricultural programs. It is noteworthy that the larger low-income countries with viable governments are resisting this policy. Small countries, especially those with weak governments, are unable to counteract the adverse production effects of this policy. They accordingly forego the more ample supply of food that overall modernization of agriculture would bring forth.

It is necessary to distinguish between economic activities where governments have a comparative advantage and those activities where the market has a comparative advantage.[6]

6. See Theodore W. Schultz, "Markets, Agriculture and Inflation," L. J. Norton Lecture, University of Illinois, Urbana-Champaign, June 11, 1980.

By this test, most organized agricultural research is a function of government, and it produces primarily *public goods*.
In the United States, only 25 percent of all agricultural research is done by private firms for profit. In low-income
countries, private firms do a much smaller proportion of
such research. The USDA has a marked advantage in col-
lecting and reporting agricultural statistics. The government also has a strong comparative advantage in specifying
standards of measurement for products that are bought and
sold. It is the primary authority in determining the property
rights of the buyers and sellers of products. Inspection of
agricultural products with special emphasis on food is done
primarily by government. The maintenance of a constant
general level of prices is one of the functions of government.
In high-income countries, endeavors to reduce inequality
in the distribution of personal income are mainly by
governments.

The comparative advantages of the market in agriculture
and in other parts of the economy are neither acknowledged
nor supported by most of the members of the International
Donor Community. Donor agencies, with few exceptions,
are strongly biased against markets. They thrive on the rhetoric of market failures. Most host governments also have a
vested interest in this bias. The international agricultural
research centers about which I have knowledge on this issue
are among the exceptions. Private foundations tend to be
ambivalent.

The comparative advantage of the price-making activity of
markets, despite the handicaps imposed by governments
and rationalized by the doctrine of market failures, continues to be demonstrable. No government that has abol-
ished markets has been successful in modernizing agriculture. The inefficiency in the allocation of resources in
agriculture in all centrally controlled economies is not in
doubt. Governments of low-income countries that procure
food grains from farmers at below market prices reduce the
economic capacities of farmers to modernize agriculture.
Governments that have nationalized the pricing of fertilizer
by controlling its import, production, and distribution have

without exception been inefficient and wasteful. The governments of many low-income countries, despite the urgent requirement for more agricultural production, underprice their agricultural products. In most of these countries, free trade and internal farm-product and input prices at prevailing international rates would be a boon for the modernization of their agriculture.

But donor agencies are in general so strongly committed to the doctrine of market failures that they are incapable of perceiving the comparative advantage of markets. The economic effect of a good deal of foreign aid is to strengthen the capacity of the host governments to discriminate against agriculture.

It should also be noted that proliferation in the United States of political groups bent on promoting government regulations to keep farmers from poisoning the soil, from contaminating streams and the water supply, from depleting cropland, from using a long list of man-made chemicals, and from destroying endangered species, provide ever more support for the doctrine of market failures. A market-oriented agriculture is viewed by these groups as an environmental and social hazard. Donor agencies, as might be expected, take full advantage of the political success of these groups. Government failures in controlling agriculture, including the failures of the donor agencies, are rarely on the agenda. It should not come as a surprise that potential agricultural production in many low-income countries is impaired by the resulting distortions in agricultural incentives.[7]

There are two additional attributes of aid agencies that call for comment. Small countries, and countries regardless of size that have weak governments, find it exceedingly difficult to cope with the vast number of donors. Bangladesh's weak government is confronted by over a hundred donor agencies. There is no way that the government can establish the public interest to be served by these donors and hold them to account in what they are doing. Kenya, which has a viable government, faces a similar problem, and recently

7. See Theodore W. Schultz, ed., *Distortions of Agricultural Incentives* (Bloomington, Ind.: Indiana University Press, 1978).

requested the International Agricultural Development Service (a foundation) to advise on how to cope with this proliferation of donor agencies. The problem is endemic among small low-income countries.

The second attribute pertains to the distortion of information that is produced and distributed by donor agencies, much of which is falsified bad news to win more financial support for the agency. Julian L. Simon cites the 1977 UN statement that "more than 100,000 West Africans perished of hunger" in the Sahel between 1968 and 1973 and shows that it is false.[8] How valid is the bad news that "14 million acres a year are vanishing as deserts spread around the globe"? The truth is exactly the opposite, as a country-by-country survey of the changes in arable land shows. A UN commission predicts "500 million starvation deaths in Asia between 1980 and 2025." It is almost gospel for the World Bank and A.I.D. that "higher population growth implies lower per capita economic growth." Here, too, there is much evidence to the contrary. The U.S. aid agency publication *Agenda* is a fountain of bad news: earth, water, and air casualties; U.S. industries wanting to dump toxic waste in the Third World; the threat of pesticides; the time-bomb in the cities; the impairment of the environment in the Third World, and on and on. The "Global Report to the President's Council on Environmental Quality" is still another example of this class.

A few economists have examined aspects of the economic effects of foreign aid.[9] Those studies that are devoted to the

8. Julian L. Simon, "Resources, Population, Environment: An Oversupply of False Bad News," *Science*, June 27, 1980, pp. 1431–37.

9. P. T. Bauer has done yeoman work on the limitations of foreign aid; see his *Dissent on Development* (Cambridge, Mass.: Harvard University Press, 1972), and "The Harm That Foreign Aid Does," *Wall Street Journal*, June 9, 1980. Harry G. Johnson also addressed himself frequently to these issues during his successful career. Uma Lele's 29-page postscript to the third printing of her *The Design of Rural Development: Lessons from Africa* (Baltimore: Johns Hopkins University Press, 1979), pp. 227–56, is a first-rate contribution. Edward Schuh's essay in my *Distortions of Agricultural Incentives* (cited above) also belongs on this list; Schuh has a major paper based on his recent work as a member of the Washington establishment which is as yet unpublished.

effects on agricultural production deal mainly with what has happened in central Africa, and give a low mark to foreign aid as it has been administered. Studies that have concentrated on the effects of foreign aid on trade tell a similar story. Particular institutional reforms (and some land reforms) also fail the economic test. My own inquiries suggest that neither donor agencies nor the host governments with which they deal know or appear to want to know the preferences and the resource constraints that determine the choices that farm people in low-income countries make. Farm people in most of these countries continue to have little or no political influence to eliminate the prevailing discrimination against agriculture. Distortions of agricultural incentives are endemic. International and domestic markets are deemed to be failures for which governmental substitutes must be developed. Most donor agencies actually do very little to improve the schooling and health of farm people. The achievements in agricultural research are an exception, mainly because of the early innovations of private foundations and because of early research programs in low-income countries by a few land-grant universities. Governmental programs designed strictly for emergency aid, however, deserve a high mark.

Farm people in low-income countries deserve a much better deal than they are receiving from the International Donor Community. Would that economists were providing the analytical foundation to bring this about.

Conclusion:
Interpretations and
Implications

Books have a way of acquiring a life of their own. Interpretations of this book will reflect the beliefs and experiences of those who read it, and for that reason they will differ from what I intended to convey. They will differ depending on whether the reader lives in a low- or a high-income country and on whether the reader believes that economics is, or is not, important in human affairs. In the event that the book survives its infancy, I am concerned about how it will be interpreted and how useful it will be after a decade or longer. My expectation is that the substance of the analysis will fare better when it is read by people in low- than by those in high-income countries. This assessment does not mean that government officials in low-income countries will take kindly to parts of it. But poor people in general, provided they can afford the book, will find it telling and useful. In high-income countries, economics tends to be suspect, and for that reason my treatment of economic distortions that impair productivity and welfare will not be readily accepted.

I do not claim that any part of this book is definitive. Each chapter is a preliminary report on issues on which I have done some thinking and research. I am keenly aware that economic analysis is beset with difficulties and that it is exceedingly hard to convey to others what one has learned. I know that economic thought is more comprehensive than is the language of economics, that this language is more comprehensive than standard economic theory, and that this theory in turn is more comprehensive than the mathematical formulations of economics. Each of these approaches, however, has its own comparative advantage.

I am neither pessimistic nor optimistic in my interpretation. I argue that the dismal view of economics associated with Malthus and Ricardo is not warranted. Malthus could not have anticipated the substitution by parents of quality for quantity of children. Nor could Ricardo have anticipated that modern research would produce substitutes for the original properties of land.

It does not distract from the economic fundamentals set forth by Adam Smith to point out that the wealth of nations would come to be predominantly the acquired abilities of people—their education, experience, skills, and health. No one at Smith's time could have foreseen that there would be a nation in which four-fifths of the national income would be derived from earnings and only a fifth of it from property. Yet the United States is such a nation. We have learned that advances in knowledge are an important source of wealth and income. We appear, however, to know less about the functions of organization than Adam Smith knew. Pessimism is warranted with regard to the adverse effects of governments on economic productivity, whereas there is much room for optimism in the observed private responses of people to economic incentives.

But there is an abundance of rhetoric consisting of dire predictions that the soils of the earth are being depleted, natural resources are being exhausted, the land that is suitable for crops cannot produce enough food for the still growing population, and that massive famines will soon occur. These predictions are not a true reckoning of the limits of the earth, because the future productivity of the economy is not foreordained by space, energy, and cropland. It will be determined by the abilities of human beings. It has been so in the past and there are no compelling reasons why it will not be so in the years to come. Increases in these acquired abilities of human beings are open-ended. Whereas there are serious doubts about the performance of governments, governments do come and go, and in this there is room for hope.

Understanding the economic dynamics of productivity and its contributions to human welfare is exceedingly important. What matters in the conduct of economic affairs is the understanding that prevails in society generally and in government in particular. Since World War II, a considerable number of low-income countries have been learning from their economic mistakes, and their understanding of their economic dynamics is improving. In some high-income countries, including the United States, there has been a decline in understanding the fundamentals of economic productivity.

I have dealt mainly with investment in people and knowledge. Investment implies the commitment of resources to acquire future income and satisfactions. It is an economic approach to the observable behavior of people and of their governments. Economic theory is robust when theory and observable evidence tell the same story. Throughout this book I have featured the evidence, with only a little elaboration of theory. Fundamental economic theory has general applicability, in the sense that it is not restricted to a particular society, culture, or country, whether small or large, poor or rich. All people are constrained by scarce resources. The things they want are not free; they thus choose to use the resources available to them that best serve their preferences. With special emphasis on investment, I have endeavored to show what is required to improve economic productivity and its contributions to the future well-being of people.

The difference between high- and low-income countries in resource constraints, and in what people can afford to consume and invest, is very large. Because of this large difference, it is exceedingly difficult for economists from high-income countries to comprehend the real implications of the severe resource constraints of low-income countries and the nature of the preferences of poor people that determine the choices they make. The government and the people of

Bangladesh, for instance, simply cannot afford the social services that the government of Sweden provides for its people.

I find much of what the high-income countries do to assist low-income countries to increase their economic productivity seriously flawed. There are three major defects. The first is a consequence of the low priority that is given to investment in human capital, i.e., investment in schooling, higher education, and health. These are high priority investments in low-income countries, and ones which they have been making on their own despite their meager incomes. The achievements of many low-income countries in their private and public investments in human capital is indeed impressive given their resource constraints.

A second flaw is the result of the social reform conditions that are attached to various forms of foreign aid. The purpose of these conditions is to make the governments of low-income countries reduce the inequality in the personal distribution of income as high-income countries are doing and can allegedly afford to do. This may be a noble objective but the programs that are used to satisfy this foreign aid condition are in general counterproductive, by virtue of the fact that they impair the potential economic productivity of the recipient countries and thus reduce the potential income available for the well-being of the people.

Probably the most costly over any extended period of time is the third flaw, which is a consequence of the pervasive bias against the role of markets. This bias is strongly entrenched in the International Donor Community and is shared by many of the governments of low-income countries. It is a bias that thrives on the rhetoric of market failure. Donor agencies acquire a vested interest in market failures. Instead of strengthening the performance of markets, what they do is to weaken them.

The class of market failures that does the most economic harm is a result of what governments do to markets. Donor agencies are frequently accessory to these failures. Foreign aid, notably in the case of aid in agricultural commodities (P.L. 480 aid) in effect contributes to the agricultural price distortions that the governments receiving such aid impose on agriculture. Where these inefficient government prices prevail, the comparative advantage of input and output market prices is lost, though free internal market prices consistent with prevailing international prices would be a boon in increasing the productivity of agriculture in many low-income countries. Such prices are one of the necessary conditions in achieving the economic potential of agricultural production in these countries.

A second major economic implication is that free internal market prices, consistent with international prices in Western European countries, Japan, and some of the other high-income countries (not taking into account the pricing that occurs in communist countries), would not only be a boon for consumers in high-income countries, but would contribute substantially to the export opportunities of a good number of low-income countries. Gains from such trade would probably contribute more to the agricultural development of low-income countries than foreign aid.

Agricultural research is an exception. Although private business firms do some agricultural research, and some private foundations have been successful innovators in supporting some agricultural research in low-income countries, by and large governments have a marked comparative advantage in organizing and supporting such research. The increase in agricultural research enterprises during recent decades is an impressive achievement. Research pertaining to health has also advanced somewhat in some low-income countries. Basic science research, however, has not fared as well.

An economic critique of the advances in population quality and in knowledge restricted to low-income countries and to the International Donor Community would be one-sided and, to some extent, unfair if no reference were made to the impairment of, for instance, the productivity of the U.S. economy by economic distortions. The distortion of schooling in large cities is a case in point. So are the distortions in basic science and economic research associated with the funding of that research by government. There are, however, all manner of other distortions. Whereas the governments of some low-income countries are improving their economic policies, in the United States the proliferation of political movements that view economics with disdain, along with apparent general public support for government market interventions, are in considerable measure contributing to the decline in the performance of the U.S. economy.

There is hope, however, provided we learn from our historical economic success. A significant measure of that success is the well over fivefold increase in real earnings per hour of work achieved between 1900 and 1970, representative of a gain in productivity that has been a profound contribution to human well-being.

Appendix: Tables A–C

Table A WAGES AND THE PRICE OF WHEAT IN THE UNITED STATES

		Bushel of Wheat	Weekly Wages	Weekly Wages in Bushels of Wheat
1817		$2.41[a]	$ 5.04[d]	2.1
1890		.97[b]	8.40[d]	8.7
1900		.67[b]	8.64[d]	12.9
1970		1.58[c]	151.60[e]	95.9
1977	(August)	2.31[c]	255.38	110

[a] *Historical Statistics of United States*, Wholesale Price, Series E–101, Wheat (Washington, D.C.: U.S. Department of Commerce, 1960).
[b] Neal Potter and Francis T. Christy, Jr., *Trends in Natural Resource Commodities* (Baltimore: Johns Hopkins University Press for Resources for the Future, 1962), p. 93, Table AP-3: Kansas City average.
[c] Hard winter wheat, Kansas City, from current USDA reports.
[d] Hourly wages of unskilled workers working 60 hours per week.
[e] Hourly wages of manufacturing production workers working 40 hours per week, including nonwage compensation which adds 13 percent to the money wages paid. From current reports of the Bureau of Labor Statistics.

Table B HOURLY WAGES OR EARNINGS OF UNSKILLED WORKERS, PUBLIC SCHOOL TEACHERS, ASSOCIATE PROFESSORS, AND MANUFACTURING PRODUCTION WORKERS IN THE UNITED STATES FOR SELECTED DATES SINCE 1900

| Year | Consumer Price Index (1967 = 100) | Unskilled Workers' Wages | | Public School Teachers' Earnings in 1967 Dollars | Associate Professors' Earnings in 1967 Dollars | Manufacturing Workers' Wages in 1967 Dollars |
		In Current Dollars	In 1967 Dollars			
1900	25	$ .144	$ .58	$ .82	$2.60	$ .60
1908	28	.182	.65	.95	2.94	.67
1910	29	.181	.62	.96	2.98	.70
1913	29.7	.198	.67	1.05	3.05	.74
1915	30.4	.212	.70	1.08	3.11	.74
1918	45.1	.426	.94	.85	2.22	.92
1919	51.8	.513	.99	...	2.11	.92
1920	60	.529	.88	.86	2.03	.92
1922	50.2	.402	.80	1.30	2.99	.90
1924	51.2	.458	.89	1.30	3.00	1.01
1926	53.0	.461	.87	1.28	2.98	.96
1930	50	.478	.96	1.49	3.36	1.06
1932	40.9	.400	.98	1.82	4.17	1.09
1934	40.1	.479	1.19	1.61	...	1.32

1940	42.0	.611	1.45	1.85	4.20	1.60
1942	48.8	.773	1.58	1.66	3.49	1.77
1950	72.1	1.19	1.65	2.30	3.60	2.15
1955	80.2	1.52	1.90	2.72	...	2.55
1960	88.7	1.83	2.06	3.28	4.57	2.85
1965	94.5	2.15	2.28	3.91	5.61	3.13
1969	109.8	2.69	2.45	4.31	6.12	3.29
1970	116.3	2.88	2.48	4.39	6.18	3.27
1972	125.3	3.30	2.63	4.65	6.15	3.44
1975	161.2	4.24	2.63	4.32	5.75	3.37

SOURCES: The wages of manufacturing production workers are Albert Rees's estimates of total compensation per hour of work in *Long Term Economic Growth, 1860–1970* (Washington, D.C.: U.S. Bureau of Economic Analysis, 1973), Appendix 2, pp. 222–23; they are updated and adjusted from 1957 to 1967 dollars. The estimates for unskilled workers, teachers, and associate professors are from Peter H. Lindert and Jeffrey G. Williamson, "Three Centuries of American Inequality," in *Research in Economic History*, ed. Paul Uselding, vol. 1, 1976, pp. 118–19, Table A-1. Beginning with 1930, the salaries of teachers are from the *Digest of Education Statistics*, 1975 ed. (Washington, D.C.: National Center for Education Statistics, 1975), Table 53, and the salaries of associate professors are from Beardsley Rumle and Sidney G. Tickon, *Teachers' Salaries Then and Now* (New York: Ford Foundation, 1955), Bulletin No. 1, p. 55, Table 3, up through 1953; from 1960 on, they are from the *Digest of Education Statistics*, 1975 ed., Table 99. Beginning with 1940, the salaries of teachers and associate professors are adjusted for fringe benefits as follows: 1940 and 1942, by 2½ percent; 1950 and 1955, by 5 percent; teachers' salaries are increased by 7½ percent for 1960 and 1965, and from then on by 10 percent; associate professors' salaries are raised by 10 percent from 1960 on. The 1900 estimate for associate professors was derived from supplementary data.

Table C WEEKLY HOURS, ANNUAL HOURS, HOURLY WAGES,
AND ANNUAL EARNINGS PER CAPITA IN THE UNITED STATES
FOR SELECTED YEARS, 1900 TO 1970

	(1) Average Weekly Hours *(Civilian Economy)*	*(2)* Average Annual Hours per Employee	*(3)* Hourly Wages in 1967 Dollars	*(4)* Annual Earnings in 1967 Dollars *(Col. 2 × Col. 3)*
1900	53.2	2766	.60	1660
1910	52.1	2705	.70	1894
1920	49.8	2584	.92	2377
1930	47.7	2477	1.06	2626
1935	42.6	2210	1.32	2917
1940	43.9	2278	1.60	3645
1945	45.7	2331	1.97	4592
1950	41.4	2141	2.15	4603
1960	40.0	2068	2.85	5894
1970	37.1	1929	3.27	6308

SOURCES: Hours worked are from *Long Term Economic Growth, 1860–1970* (Washington, D.C.: Bureau of Economic Analysis, 1973), Series B4 and B5, p. 212. Hourly wages are from Appendix: Table B.

Selected Bibliography

Works by other authors cited in the text are listed separately from writings by Theodore W. Schultz relevant to the issues discussed in this book.

WORKS BY OTHER AUTHORS CITED IN THE TEXT

Anderson, Arnold C., and Bowman, Mary Jean. "Education and Economic Modernization in Historical Perspective." In *Schooling and Society: Studies in the History of Education*, edited by Lawrence Stone, pp. 3–19. Baltimore: Johns Hopkins University Press, 1976.

Astin, Alexander W.; King, Margo R.; and Richardson, Gerald T. *The American Freshman: Norms for Fall, 1978*. Los Angeles: Graduate School of Education, University of California, Los Angeles, 1979.

Atkinson, Richard C. "Federal Support in the Social Sciences." *Science*, Feb. 22, 1980, p. 829.

Barlow, Robin. "The Economic Effects of Malaria Eradication." *American Economic Review* 57 (May 1967): 130–48.

Bauer, P. T. *Dissent on Development*. Cambridge, Mass.: Harvard University Press, 1972.

———. "The Harm That Foreign Aid Does." *Wall Street Journal*, June 9, 1980, editorial page.

Becker, Gary S. "A Theory of the Allocation of Time." *Economic Journal* 75 (Sept. 1963): 493–517.

———. *Human Capital: A Theoretical and Empirical Analysis with Special Reference to Education*. New York: National Bureau of Economic Research and Columbia University Press, 1964.

———. *The Economic Approach to Human Behavior, Schooling, Experience and Earnings*. New York: National Bureau of Economic Research and Columbia University Press, 1974.

Bibliography prepared by John M. Letiche.

————. "A Theory of Social Interaction." *Journal of Political Economy* 82 (Nov.–Dec. 1974): 1063–93.

————, and Lewis, H. Gregg. "Interaction Between Quantity and Quality of Children." In *Economics of the Family: Marriage, Children, and Human Capital*, edited by Theodore W. Schultz, pp. 81–90. Chicago: University of Chicago Press, 1974.

————, and Tomes, Nigel. "Child Endowments and the Quantity and Quality of Children." *Journal of Political Economy* 84, pt. 2 (August 1976): S143–S162.

Behrman, Jere. *Supply Response in Underdeveloped Agriculture: A Case Study of Four Major Annual Crops in Thailand, 1937–63.* Amsterdam: North Holland Publishing Co., 1967.

Blaug, Mark. "Educational Policy and the Economics of Education: Some Practical Lessons for Educational Planners in Developing Countries." In *Education and Development Reconsidered*, edited by F. Champion Ward, pp. 23–32. New York: Praeger Publishers, 1974.

Borkar, G. *Health in Independent India.* New Delhi: Ministry of Health, Government of India, 1957.

Bowman, Mary Jean. "The Land-Grant Colleges and Universities in Human Resource Development." *Journal of Economic History* 22 (Dec. 1962): 523–46.

————, and Anderson, C. Arnold. "Theoretical Considerations in Educational Planning." In *Education Planning*, edited by Don Adams, pp. 4–47. Syracuse, N.Y.: Syracuse University Press, 1964.

Boyce, James K., and Evenson, Robert E. *National and International Agricultural Research and Extension Programs.* New York: Agricultural Development Council, 1975.

Butz, William P., and Habicht, Jean-Pierre. "The Effects of Nutrition and Health on Fertility." In *Population and Development*, edited by Ronald G. Ridker. Baltimore: Johns Hopkins University Press, 1976.

Carnegie Commission on Higher Education. *A Classification of Institutions of Higher Education.* A technical report. Berkeley, Calif., 1973.

Dalrymple, Dana G. *Development and Spread of High Yielding Varieties of Wheat and Rice in the Less Developed Nations.* USDA Foreign Agricultural Economic Report No. 95. Washington, D.C.: USDA, 1978.

Debeauvais, Michel. "The Contribution of the Economics of Education to Aid Policies: A Critical Comment." In *Education and Development Reconsidered*, edited by F. Champion Ward. New York: Praeger Publishers, 1974.

De Tray, Dennis N. "The Substitution Between Quantity and Quality of Children in the Household." Ph.D. dissertation, University of Chicago, 1972.

————. "Child Quality and the Demand for Children." In *Economics of the Family: Marriage, Children, and Human Capital*, edited by Theodore W. Schultz, pp. 91–114. Chicago: University of Chicago Press, 1974.

————. *Child Schooling and Family Size*. Santa Monica, Calif.: RAND Corp., April 1978.

Economic Report of the President. Washington, D.C.: Council of Economic Advisors, 1976.

Evenson, Robert E. "The Organization of Research to Improve Crops and Animals in Low-Income Countries." In *Distortions of Agricultural Incentives*, edited by Theodore W. Schultz, pp. 223–45. Bloomington, Ind.: Indiana University Press, 1978.

————, and Kislev, Yoav. *Agricultural Research and Productivity*. New Haven, Conn.: Yale University Press, 1975.

Government of India Planning Commission. *Draft Five Year Plan, 1978–83*. New Delhi, 1978.

Griliches, Zvi. "Research Costs and Social Returns: Hybrid Corn and Related Innovations." *Journal of Political Economy* 66 (October 1958): 419–31.

Grossman, M. *The Demand for Health*. New York: Columbia University Press, 1972.

Hardin, Charles M. "Conflicting Views on the World Food Problem—A Socialist or Capitalist Orientation: Which is Preferable?" Mimeographed. Davis, Calif.: University of California, Davis, November 1978.

Hayek, F. A. "The Dilemma of Specialization." In *The State of the Social Sciences*. Chicago: University of Chicago Press, 1956.

Hicks, John. *Capital and Growth*. Oxford: Oxford University Press, 1965.

Hill, Russell C., and Stafford, Frank P. "The Allocation of Time to Preschool Children and Educational Opportunity." *Journal of Human Resources* 9 (Summer 1974): 323–41.

Johnson, D. Gale. "Food Production Potentials in Developing Countries: Will They be Realized?" Bureau of Economic Studies Occasional Paper No. 1. St. Paul, Minn.: Macalester College, 1977.

————. "International Prices and Trade in Reducing the Distortions of Incentives." In *Distortions of Agricultural Incentives*, edited by Theodore W. Schultz, pp. 195–215. Bloomington, Ind.: Indiana University Press, 1978.

————. "The World Food Situation: Recent Developments and Prospects." University of Chicago, Graduate School of Business, 1978.

————. "The World Food Situation: Developments During the 1970s and Prospects for the 1980s." University of Chicago Agricultural Economics Research Paper No. 80–10, March 1980.

Johnson, Harry G. "Toward a Generalized Capital Accumulation Approach to Economic Development." In *The Residual Factor and Economic Growth.* Paris: OECD, 1964.

————. *On Economics and Society.* Chicago: University of Chicago Press, 1975.

Knight, Frank. "Diminishing Returns from Investment." *Journal of Political Economy* 52 (March 1944): 26–47.

Kothari, V. N. "Factor Cost of Education in India." *Indian Economic Journal* 13 (April–June 1966): 631–46.

————. "Disparities in Relative Earnings Among Different Countries." *Economic Journal* 80 (Sept. 1970): 605–6.

Krutilla, John V., and Fisher, Anthony C. *The Economics of the Natural Environments.* Baltimore: Johns Hopkins University Press for Resources for the Future, 1975.

Kuznets, Simon. "Economic Growth and Income Inequality." *American Economic Review* 45 (March 1955): 1–28.

————. "Quantitative Aspects of the Economic Growth of Nations: VIII. Distribution of Income by Size." *Economic Development and Cultural Change* 11 (II) (Jan. 1963): 1–80.

————. *Modern Economic Growth.* New Haven, Conn.: Yale University Press, 1966.

————. *Economic Growth and Nations.* Cambridge, Mass.: Harvard University Press, 1971.

Leibowitz, Arleen. "Home Investment in Children." In *Economics of the Family: Marriage, Children, and Human Capital,* edited by Theodore W. Schultz. Chicago: University of Chicago Press, 1974.

Lele, Uma. *The Design of Rural Development: Lessons from Africa.* Baltimore: Johns Hopkins University Press, 1979.

Leontief, W. "Introduction to a Theory of the Internal Structure of Functional Relationships." *Econometrica* 15 (Oct. 1947): 361–73.

Lindert, Peter H. "Land Scarcity and American Growth." *Journal of Economic History* 34 (1974): 851–84.

Macchiarola, Frank J. "Mid-Year Report of the Chancellor of the Schools for New York City Board of Education." Mimeographed. Jan. 1979.

Makhija, Indra. "The Economic Contribution of Children and Its Effects on Fertility and Schooling: Rural India." Ph.D. dissertation, University of Chicago, 1977.

Malenbaum, Wilfred. "Health and Productivity in Poor Areas." In *Empirical Studies in Health Economics,* edited by H. E. Klarman. Baltimore: Johns Hopkins University Press, 1970.

Mann, Dale. *The Politics of Administrative Representation.* Lexington, Mass.: D. C. Heath and Company, Lexington Books, 1976.

Marshall, Alfred. *Principles of Economics.* 8th ed. New York: Macmillan, 1920.

Marshall, Eliot. "Defense." *Science,* Feb. 8, 1980, pp. 619–20.

Mincer, Jacob. "On-the-Job Training: Costs, Returns, and Some Implications." In *Investment in Human Beings*, edited by Theodore W. Schultz. Supplement to the *Journal of Political Economy* 70 (Oct. 1962): 50–79.

National Research Council, National Academy of Sciences. *Evaluating Federal Support of Poverty Research*. Paperback reprint, Cambridge, Mass.: Schenkman Publishing Co., 1979.

National Science Foundation. *National Patterns of R and D Resources*. NSF–78–313. Washington, D.C., 1978.

Nerlove, Marc. "Toward a New Theory of Population and Economic Growth." In *Economics of the Family: Marriage, Children, and Human Capital*, edited by Theodore W. Schultz, pp. 527–45. Chicago: University of Chicago Press, 1974.

Nolting, L. E., and Feshback, M. "R and D Employment in the U.S.S.R." *Science*, Feb. 1, 1980, pp. 493–503.

Palmer, Archie M., ed. *Research Centers Directory*. 6th ed. Detroit: Gale Research Company, 1979.

Panchamukhi, P. R. "Educational Capital in India." *Indian Economic Journal* 12 (Jan.–March 1965): 306–14.

Patton, Carl V., and Marver, James D. "The Correlates of Consultation: American Academics in the 'Real World.'" *Higher Education* 5 (August 1976): 319–35.

———. "Paid Consulting by American Academics." *Educational Record* 60 (Spring 1979): 175–84.

Piel, Gerard. "On Promoting Useful Knowledge." *Proceedings of the American Philosophical Society*, Dec. 28, 1979, pp. 337–40.

Potter, Neal, and Christy, Francis T., Jr. *Trends in Natural Resource Commodities*. Baltimore: Johns Hopkins University Press for Resources for the Future, 1962.

Psacharopoulos, George. "Educational Planning: Past and Present." *Prospects* 8, no. 2 (1978): 135–42.

Ram, Rati. "India's Agriculture During 1950–70: An Exercise in Growth Source Analysis." University of Chicago Agricultural Economics Paper 74–14. 1974.

———, and Schultz, Theodore W. "Life Span, Health, Savings, and Productivity." *Economic Development and Cultural Change* 27 (April 1979): 399–421.

Rees, Albert. "Pattern of Wages, Prices and Productivity." In *Wages, Prices, Profits, and Productivity*, pp. 11–37. Proceedings of the American Assembly. New York: Columbia University Press, June 1959.

Rosenzweig, Mark R., and Evenson, Robert E. "Fertility, Schooling and the Economic Contribution of Children in Rural India: An Econometric Analysis." *Econometrica* 45 (July 1977): 1065–79.

Rosenzweig, Mark R., and Wolpin, Kenneth I. "Testing the Quantity-Quality Fertility Model: The Use of Twins as a Natural Experiment." Mimeographed. New Haven: Yale University Economic Growth Center, October 1978.

Rudolph, Susanne Hoeber, and Rudolph, Lloyd I. *Education and Politics in India.* Cambridge, Mass.: Harvard University Press, 1972.

Ruttan, Vernon W. *Integrated Rural Development Programs: A Skeptical Perspective.* New York: Agricultural Development Council, 1975. Reprinted from *International Development Review* 17, no. 4 (1975).

Shah, C. H. "Food Preferences and Nutrition: A Perspective on Poverty in Less Developed Countries." *Indian Journal of Agricultural Economics* 35 (January–March 1980): 1–39.

Sher, Jonathan P., and Tompkins, Rachel B. "Economy, Efficiency and Equality." Washington, D.C.: National Institute of Education, July 1976.

Shils, Edward. "The Conflict of God and Caesar." The second of three 1979 Jefferson Lectures. University of Chicago, April 10, 1979.

Shortlidge, Robert L., Jr. "A Social-Economic Model of School Attendance in Rural India." Department of Agricultural Economics Occasional Paper No. 86. Ithaca, N.Y.: Cornell University, January 1976.

Simon, Julian L. "Resources, Population, Environment: An Oversupply of False Bad News." *Science,* June 27, 1980, pp. 1431–37.

Sjaastad, Larry A. "The Costs and Returns of Human Migration." In *Investment in Human Beings,* edited by Theodore W. Schultz. Supplement to the *Journal of Political Economy* 70 (Oct. 1962): 80–93.

Sovani, N. V. *Population Trends and Agriculture Development: Case Studies of Sri Lanka and India.* United Nations Economic and Social Council Paper E/Conf. 60/SYM 1/11. New York, April 1973.

Sukhatme, P. V. "Malnutrition and Poverty." Ninth Lal Bahadur Shastri Memorial Lecture, Indian Agricultural Research Institute, New Delhi, January 29, 1977.

United States Bureau of Economic Analysis. *Long Term Economic Growth 1860–1970.* Washington, D.C., 1973.

United States Department of Health, Education and Welfare. *Digest of Education Statistics 1977–78.* Washington, D.C.: National Center for Education Statistics, 1978.

Usher, Dan. "An Imputation to the Measure of Economic Growth for Changes in Life Expectancy." In *The Measurement of Economic and Social Performance,* edited by Milton Moss. New York: National Bureau of Economic Research, 1978.

Viner, Jacob. *The Role of Providence in the Social Order: An Essay in Intellectual History.* Philadelphia: American Philosophical

Society, 1972; paperback ed. Princeton, N.J.: Princeton University Press, 1976.

———. *Religious Thought and Economic Society: Four Chapters of an Unfinished Work*, edited by Jacques Melitz and Donald Winch. Durham, N.C.: Duke University Press, 1978.

Walsh, John. "Does High School Grade Inflation Mask a More Alarming Trend?" *Science*, March 9, 1979, p. 982.

Welch, Finis. "Education in Production." *Journal of Political Economy* 78 (Jan.–Feb. 1970): 35–59.

———. "The Role of Investments in Human Capital in Agriculture." In *Distortions of Agricultural Incentives*, edited by Theodore W. Schultz, pp. 259–81. Bloomington, Ind.: Indiana University Press, 1978.

Williams, Alan. "Health Service Planning." In *Studies in Modern Economic Analysis*, edited by M. J. Artis and A. R. Nobay. Edinburgh: Blackwell, 1977.

Wilson, John T. "Higher Education and the Washington Scene: 1980." Mimeographed. University of Chicago, October 1979.

Winslow, C. E. A. *The Cost of Sickness and the Price of Health.* Geneva: World Health Organization, 1951.

World Bank Atlas: Population, Per Capita Product and Growth Rates. Washington, D.C.: World Bank, 1974.

World Bank. *Health: Sector Working Paper.* Washington, D.C., 1975.

SELECT LIST OF WRITINGS BY THEODORE W. SCHULTZ

Books

Training and Recruiting of Personnel in the Rural Social Sciences. With L. Witt. Washington, D.C.: American Council of Education, 1941.

Redirecting Farm Policy. New York: Macmillan Co., 1943.

Agriculture in an Unstable Economy. New York: McGraw-Hill, 1945.

Production and Welfare of Agriculture. New York: Macmillan Co., 1949.

Measures for Economic Development of Underdeveloped Countries. With D. R. Gadgil, Arthur Lewis, George Hakim, and Alberto Baltra Cortez. New York: United Nations Department of Economic Affairs, 1951.

The Economic Organization of Agriculture. New York: McGraw-Hill, 1953.

The Economic Value of Education. New York: Columbia University Press, 1963.

Transforming Traditional Agriculture. New Haven, Conn.: Yale University Press, 1964. Reprinted New York: Arno Press, 1976.

Economic Crises in World Agriculture. Ann Arbor: University of Michigan Press, 1965.

Economic Growth and Agriculture. New York: McGraw-Hill, 1968.

Investments in Human Capital: The Role of Education and of Research. New York: Macmillan Co., Free Press, 1971.

Human Resources. NBER Fiftieth Anniversary Colloquium 6. New York: National Bureau of Economic Research and Columbia University Press, 1972.

Symposia

Food for the World. Chicago: University of Chicago Press, 1945. Reprinted New York: Arno Press, 1976.

Investment in Human Beings. Supplement to the *Journal of Political Economy* 70 (Oct. 1962).

Investment in Education: The Equity-Efficiency Quandary. Supplement to the *Journal of Political Economy* 80 (May–June 1972).

New Economic Approaches to Fertility. Supplement to the *Journal of Political Economy* 81 (March–April 1973).

Marriage, Family Human Capital, and Fertility. Supplement to the *Journal of Political Economy* 82 (March–April 1974).

Economics of the Family: Marriage, Children, and Human Capital. Chicago: University of Chicago Press for the National Bureau of Economic Research, 1975.

Distortions of Agricultural Incentives. Bloomington, Ind.: Indiana University Press, 1978.

Articles and Papers

"Diminishing Returns in View of Progress in Agricultural Production." *Journal of Farm Economics* 14 (Oct. 1932): 640–49.

"Some Notes on International Trade." *Agricultural Economic Facts,* Ames, Iowa, report 4 (April 1932).

"Trade and Tariff Problems Related to Agriculture." In *Commission of Inquiry into National Policy in International Economic Relations.* Minneapolis: University of Minnesota Press, 1934.

"Agriculture's Share of National Income and the Role of Cooperatives." *American Cooperative,* 1937, pp. 143–48.

"Economic Aspects of New Industrial Outlets for Agricultural Products." *Journal of Farm Economics* 20 (Feb. 1938): 134–39.

"Future Production Programs and Price Policies for Agriculture." In *Proceedings* of conference *What Is a Desirable National Agricultural Program!* University of Illinois Extension Service, 1938.

"Scope and Method in Agricultural Economic Research." *Journal of Political Economy* 47 (Oct. 1939): 705–17.

"The Theory of Firm and Farm Management Research." *Journal of Farm Economics* 21 (Aug. 1939): 570–86.

"Agriculture and the National Economy." In *Proceedings* of Iowa Farm Bureau Federation. Des Moines, 1939.

"Capital Rationing, Uncertainty, and Farm Tenancy Reform." *Journal of Political Economy* 48 (June 1940): 309–24.

"Needed Additions to the Theoretical Equipment of an Agricultural Economist." *Journal of Farm Economics* 22 (Feb. 1940): 60–62.

"Economic Effects of Agricultural Programs." *American Economic Review* 30 (Feb. 1941): 127–54.

Farm Prices for Food Production. Wartime Farm and Food Policy pamphlet no. 2. Ames, Iowa: Iowa State College Press, 1943.

"Two Conditions Necessary for Economic Progress in Agriculture." *Canadian Journal of Economics and Political Science* 10 (Aug. 1944): 298–311.

"Transition Readjustments in Agriculture." *Journal of Farm Economics* 26 (Feb. 1944): 77–88.

"Food Supply and Nutrition in a Developing Economy." *Journal of Home Economics* 36 (Sept. 1944): 405–08.

"Farm Income, Migration, and Leisure." *Proceedings* of Institute on Library Extension. University of Chicago Graduate Library School, 1944.

"Food and Agriculture in a Developing Economy." In *Food for the World*, edited by T. W. Schultz, pp. 306–20. Chicago: University of Chicago Press, 1945.

"Income Accounting to Guide Production and Welfare Policies." In *Proceedings* of the Western Farm Economics Association, pp. 58–66, 1945.

"Postwar Agricultural Policy: A Review of the Land-Grant Colleges Report." *The Journal of Land and Public Utility Economics* 21 (May 1945): 95–107.

"Changes in Economic Structure Affecting American Agriculture." *Journal of Farm Economics* 28 (Feb. 1946): 15–27.

"Production and Welfare Objectives for American Agriculture." *Journal of Farm Economics* 28 (May 1946): 444–57.

"Effects of Employment upon Factor Costs in Agriculture." *Journal of Farm Economics* 29 (Nov. 1947): 1122–32.

"The Economic Stability of American Agriculture." *Journal of Farm Economics* 29 (Nov. 1947): 809–26.

"Food, Agriculture, and Trade." *Journal of Farm Economics* 29 (Feb. 1947): 1–19.

"The Public Lands and National Economy." In *Symposium on the*

Public Lands. University of New Mexico. Albuquerque, N. Mex., Oct. 1947.

"The Economic Challenge that Comes with Full Production." In *Proceedings* of the 3rd National Forum of Agriculture, Labor and Industry, University of Wyoming. Laramie, Wyo., July 1947.

"Supporting Agricultural Prices by Concealed Dumping." *Journal of Political Economy* 56 (April 1948): 157–60.

"Spot and Future Prices as Production Guides." *American Economic Review* 39 (May 1949): 135–49.

"Agricultural Price Policy." *Proceedings of the Academy of Political Science* 23 (Jan. 1949): 12–21.

"Effects of Trade and Industrial Output of Western Germany upon Agriculture." *American Economic Review* 40 (May 1950): 522–30.

"Reflections on Poverty within Agriculture." *Journal of Political Economy* 43 (Feb. 1950): 1–15.

"A Frame of Reference for Analyzing Income and Price Policies." In *Educational and Methods Conference in Public Support*, pp. 52–53. Chicago: The Farm Foundation, 1950.

"A Theory of Policy Making Based on Regrets (And Some Observations on Price Policy Research)." In *Proceedings* of the New England Research Council on Marketing and Food Supply. Boston, Mass., April 1950.

"Declining Economic Importance of Agricultural Land." *Economic Journal* 61 (Dec. 1951): 725–40.

"Economic Efficiency: Its Meaning, Measurement and Application to Agricultural Problems." *Journal of Farm Economics* 33 (Feb. 1951): 115–19.

"Policy Lessons from the Economic Mobilization of the United States." *Journal of Political Economy* 31 (Nov. 1951): 613–20.

"A Framework for Land Economics—the Long View." *Journal of Farm Economics* 33 (May 1951): 204–15.

"The Supply of Food in Relation to Economic Development." *Economic Development and Cultural Change* 1 (Dec. 1952): 244–49.

"The Instability of Farm Prices Reconsidered." *Journal of Farm Economics* 36 (Dec. 1954): 777–89.

"A Guide to Better Policy for Agriculture." *Consumer Reports* 19 (April 1954): 185–89.

"Some Guiding Principles in Organizing Agricultural Economics Research." *Journal of Farm Economics* 36 (Feb. 1954): 18–21.

"The Contribution of the Economist to Programs of Technical Development." In *Proceedings* of the Ninth International Conference of Agricultural Economists, pp. 470–82. London: Oxford University Press, 1956.

The Economic Test in Latin America. Cornell University Bulletin No. 35. Ithaca, N.Y.: Cornell University, August 1956.

"The Role of the Government in Promoting Economic Growth." In *The State of the Social Sciences*, edited by Leonard D. White, pp. 372–83. Chicago: University of Chicago Press, 1956.

"Latin American Economic Policy Lessons." *American Economic Review* 46 (May 1956): 425–32.

"Reflections on Agricultural Production, Output and Supply." *Journal of Farm Economics* 38 (Aug. 1956): 746–62.

"An Alternate Diagnosis of the Farm Problem." *Journal of Farm Economics* 38 (Dec. 1956): 1137–52.

"Lessons for Agricultural Economics from U.S.A. Experiences." *Indian Journal of Agricultural Economics* 11, no. 1 (1956): 9–13.

"Agriculture and the Application of Knowledge." In *A Look to the Future*. Battle Creek, Mich.: W. K. Kellogg Foundation, 1956.

"Output-Input Relationships Revisited." *Journal of Farm Economics* 40 (Nov. 1958): 924–32.

"The Emerging Economic Scene and Its Relation to High School Education." In *The High School in a New Era*, edited by Francis S. Chase and Harold A. Anderson, pp. 97–109. Chicago: University of Chicago Press, 1958.

"Human Wealth and Economic Growth." *The Humanist* 19, no. 2 (1959): 71–81.

"A Foreign Economic Policy for What?" *Saturday Review*, Jan. 17, 1959, pp. 33–37.

"Agricultural Policy for What?" *Journal of Farm Economics* 41 (1959): 189–93.

"Investment in Man: An Economist's View." *Social Service Review* 33 (June 1959): 109–17.

"A New Era for Agriculture in Economic Growth." *The Indian Journal of Agricultural Economics* 14, no. 4 (1959): 37–43.

"Land in Economic Growth." In *Modern Land Policy*, edited by H. Halcrew, pp. 17–39. Chicago: University of Illinois Press, 1959.

"Omission of Variables, Weak Aggregates, and Fragmentation in Policy and Adjustment Studies." In *Problems and Policies of American Agriculture*, pp. 189–203. Ames, Iowa: Iowa State University Press, 1959.

"Capital Formation by Education." *Journal of Political Economy* 68 (Dec. 1960): 571–83.

"Value of U.S. Farm Surpluses to Underdeveloped Countries." *Journal of Farm Economics* 42 (Dec. 1960): 1018–30.

"Investment in Human Capital." *American Economic Review* 51 (Mar. 1961): 1–17.

"Investment in Human Capital: A Reply." *American Economic Review* 51 (Dec. 1961): 1035–39.

"A Policy to Redistribute Losses from Economic Progress." *Journal of Farm Economics* 43 (Aug. 1961): 554–65.

"U.S. Endeavors to Assist Low-Income Countries Improve Economic Capabilities of their People." *Journal of Farm Economics* 43 (Dec. 1961): 1068–78.

"Education and Economic Growth." In *Social Forces Influencing American Education*, edited by N. B. Henry, pp. 46–88. Chicago: National Society for Study of Education, 1961.

"Economic Policy Research for Agriculture." *Canadian Journal of Agricultural Economics* 9 (1961): 94–106.

"Economic Prospects of Primary Products." In *Economic Development for Latin America*, edited by H. S. Ellis, pp. 308–41. London: Macmillan; New York: St. Martin's Press, 1961.

"Connections between Natural Resources and Economic Growth." In *Natural Resources and Economic Growth*, edited by J. J. Spengler, pp. 1–9. Washington, D.C.: Resources for the Future, 1961.

"Tobin's National Goals and Economic Policy." In *Farm Policy Review Conference.* Raleigh, N.C.: North Carolina State College, 1961.

"Human Capital: Growing Asset." *Saturday Review*, Jan. 21, 1961, pp. 37–39.

"Reflections on Investment in Man." *Journal of Political Economy* 70, no. 5, pt. 2 (Oct. 1962): 1–8.

"Science and Agriculture." Report of the President's Science Advisory Committee. Washington, D.C., 1962.

"Investment in Human Capital in Poor Countries." In *Foreign Trade and Human Capital*, edited by Paul D. Zook, pp. 3–15. Dallas, Tex.: Southern Methodist University Press, 1962.

"Education as a Source of Economic Growth." Mimeographed. UNESCO Conference on Education and Economic and Social Development in Latin America. Santiago, Chile, 1962.

"Rise in the Capital Stock Represented by Education in the United States between 1900 to 1957." In *The Economics of Higher Education and Welfare*, edited by Selma G. Mushkin, pp. 93–101. Washington, D.C.: Office of Education, 1962.

"Education and Values Conducive to Economic Goals." In *Agricultural Policy Review* 2 (1962): 4–6.

"Discussion: Student Loan Programs." *Harvard Educational Review* 33 (1963): 369–70.

"National Security, Economic Growth, Individual Freedom and Agricultural Policy." In "Our Rural Problems in their Natural Setting," pp. 1–8. Mimeographed. Ames, Iowa: Iowa State University, 1963.

"Underinvestment in the Quality of Schooling: The Rural Farm Areas." In *Increasing Understanding of Public Problems and Policies, 1964*, pp. 12–34. Chicago: Farm Foundation, 1964.

"Some Economic Issues in Improving the Quality in Education." In

A Financial Program for Today's Schools, pp. 32–37. Proceedings of the Seventh National Conference on School Finance. Washington, D.C.: National Education Association, 1964.

"Our Welfare State and the Welfare of Farm People." *The Social Service Review* 38 (June 1964): 123–29.

"Economic Growth from Traditional Agriculture." In *Agricultural Sciences for the Developing Nations*, pp. 185–205. American Association for the Advancement of Science Publication No. 76. Washington, D.C.: American Association for the Advancement of Science, 1964.

"Changing Relevance of Agricultural Economics." *Journal of Farm Economics* 46 (Dec. 1964): 1004–14.

"Family Planning." *Proceedings of the White House Conference on Health*, pp. 546–48. Washington, D.C., 1965.

"Investing in Poor People: An Economist's View." *American Economic Review* 40 (May 1965): 510–20.

"Reflections on Teaching and Learning in Colleges of Agriculture." *Journal of Farm Economics* 47 (Feb. 1965): 17–22.

"Economic Basis for a New Agricultural Policy Consensus." In *Our Stake in Commercial Agriculture, Rural Poverty and World Trade*. Proceedings of the Fifth Annual Farm Policy Review Conference, Washington, D.C., 1965.

"Public Approaches to Minimize Poverty." In *Poverty amid Affluence*, edited by Leo Fishman, pp. 165–81. New Haven, Conn.: Yale University Press, 1966.

"Urban Development and Policy Implications for Agriculture." *Economic Development and Cultural Change* 15 (1966): 1–9.

"Increasing World Food Supplies: The Economic Requirements." *Proceedings of the National Academy of Sciences* 56 (1966): 322–27.

"Economic Opportunities in the World of Agriculture." In *Record of Proceedings of the Global Meeting of the Resident Representatives of the United Nations Development Program*. New York, 1966.

"Transforming Traditional Agriculture: Reply." *Journal of Farm Economics* 48, no. 4, pt. 1 (1966): 1015–18.

"Agricultural Development: The Necessary Conditions." *Agricultural Policy Review* 6, no. 4 (1966): 6–7.

Investment in Poor People. Washington, D.C.: U.S. Department of Labor, Manpower Administration, 1967.

"U.S. Mal-investments in Food for the World." In *Alternatives for Balancing Future World Food Production and Needs*, pp. 224–42. Ames: Iowa State University Center for Agricultural and Economic Development, 1967.

"Significance of India's 1918–1919 Losses of Agricultural Labour—A Reply." *Economic Journal* 77 (March 1967): 161–63.

"Education and Research in Rural Development in Latin America."
In *Rural Development in Tropical Latin America*, edited by K. L.
Turk and L. V. Crowder, pp. 391–402. Ithaca, N.Y.: Cornell University Press, 1967.

"The Latifundia Puzzle of Professor Schultz: Reply." *Journal of Farm Economics* 49 (May 1967): 511–14.

"Efficient Allocation of Brains in Modernizing World Agriculture."
Journal of Farm Economics 49 (Dec. 1967): 1071–82.

"Economic Growth Theory and Profit in Latin American Farming."
In *Agricultural Development in Latin America: The Next Decade*, pp. 169–88. Washington, D.C.: Inter-American Development Bank, 1967.

"A Missing Link in Growth Theory." In T. W. Schultz, *Economic Growth and Agriculture*, pp. 293–98. New York: McGraw-Hill, 1968.

"National Employment, Skills, and Earnings of Farm Labor." In
Farm Labor in the United States, edited by C. E. Bishop, pp.
53–69. New York: Columbia University Press, 1967.

"An Endeavor to Clarify the Economic Components Underlying
Chilean Agriculture." In *Agricultural Development in Latin
America: The Next Decade*. Washington, D.C.: Inter-American
Development Bank, April 1967.

"The Rate of Return in Allocating Investment Resources to Education." *Journal of Human Resources* 2 (Summer 1967): 293–309.

"Food for the World: Economic Implications and Opportunities." In
Proceedings of the Ninth Agricultural Industries Forum, pp.
1–14. Urbana, Ill.: University of Illinois, Department of Agricultural Economics, 1967.

"Resource Allocation in Traditional Agriculture: Reply." *Journal of
Farm Economics* 49 (Nov. 1967): 933–35.

"On the Economic Importance of Land: Reply." *Journal of Farm
Economics* 49 (Aug. 1967): 735–36.

"Institutions and the Rising Economic Value of Man." *American
Journal of Agricultural Economics* 50 (Dec. 1968): 1113–22.

"Human Capital." *International Encyclopedia of Social Sciences*.
New York: Macmillan Co., 1968.

"Resources for Higher Education: An Economist's View." *Journal
of Political Economy* 76 (May–June 1968): 327–47.

"Production Opportunities in Asian Agriculture: An Economist's
Agenda." In *Development and Change in Traditional Agriculture: Focus on South Asia*, pp. 1–8. East Lansing, Mich.: Michigan State University, Asian Studies Center, 1968.

"World Agriculture in Relation to Population, Science, Economic
Disequilibrium and Income Inequality: Reflections and Unsettled Questions." *Proceedings of the 13th International Conference of Agricultural Economists*, pp. 130–40. 1969.

"New Evidence on Farmer Responses to Economic Opportunities from the Early Agrarian History of Western Europe." In *Subsistence Agriculture and Economic Development*, edited by Clifton R. Wharton, pp. 105–10. Chicago: Aldine Publishing Co., 1969.

"Agricultural Modernization Altering World Food and Feed Grain Competition." In *International Conference on Mechanized Dryland Farming*, edited by W. C. Burronni et al., pp. 297–306. John Deere & Co., 1970.

"Some Economic Aspects of the Northland." In *Canadian Economic Problems and Policy*, edited by E. Laurence and D. Smith, pp. 352–58. New York: McGraw-Hill, 1970.

"The Human Capital Approach to Education." Chapter 2 of *Economic Factors Affecting the Financing of Education in the Decade Ahead*, edited by R. L. Johns et al. Iowa City, Iowa: National Educational Finance Project, 1970.

"The Reckoning of Education as Human Capital." In *Education, Income, and Human Capital*, edited by W. Lee Hansen, pp. 297–306. New York: National Bureau of Economic Research, 1970.

"Discussion of Extent of Gaps between Plans and Realization." In *Economic Models and Quantitative Methods for Decisions and Planning in Agriculture*, edited by Earl O. Heady, pp. 479–81. Ames, Iowa: Iowa State University Press, 1971.

"Possibilities for Improving Rural Living: An Economist's View." In *The Quality of Rural Living*, pp. 64–70. Washington, D.C.: National Academy of Sciences, 1971.

"The Food Supply—Population Growth Quandary." In National Academy of Science, *Rapid Population Growth: Consequences and Policy Implications*, pp. 245–72. Baltimore: Johns Hopkins University Press, 1971.

Education and Productivity. Prepared for the National Commission on Productivity. Washington, D.C.: U.S. Government Printing Office, 1971.

"Production Opportunities in Asian Agriculture." In *Readings in Economic Development*, edited by W. Johnson. Cincinnati: South-Western Publishing Co., 1971.

"Optimal Investment in College Instruction: Equity and Efficiency." *Journal of Political Economy* 80, no. 3, pt. 2 (May–June 1972): S2–S30.

"Knowledge, Agriculture and Welfare." In *Proceedings: Twenty-First Pugwash Conference on Science and World Affairs*, pp. 343–53. London: Taylor & Francis, 1972.

"The Role of Pugwash in Development: An Economist's View." *Proceedings: Twenty-First Pugwash Conference on Science and World Affairs*, pp. 353–55. London: Taylor & Francis, 1972.

"Woman's New Economic Commandment." In *Families of the Fu-*

ture, pp. 79–88. Ames, Iowa: Iowa State University Press, 1972.

"The Increasing Economic Value of Human Time." *American Journal of Agricultural Economics* 54 (Dec. 1972): 843–50.

"A Guide to Investors in Education with Special Reference to Developing Countries." In *Bellagio Papers*, vol. 1, edited by F. Champion Ward, pp. 82–93. New York: Praeger Publishers for the Rockefeller and Ford Foundations, 1972.

"The Value of Children: An Economic Perspective." *Journal of Political Economy* 81, no. 2, pt. 2 (March–April 1973): S2–S13.

"The Education of Farm People: An Economic Perspective." In the 1973/74 *World Year Book of Education*, pp. 50–68. London: Evans Brothers, 1973.

"The High Value of Human Time: Population Equilibrium." *Journal of Political Economy* 82, no. 2, pt. 2 (March–April 1974): S2–S10.

"Is Modern Agriculture Consistent with a Stable Environment?" In *The Future of Agriculture: Technology, Policies and Adjustment*, Proceedings of the Fifteenth International Conference of Agricultural Economists, São Paulo, Brazil, pp. 235–42. Oxford: Oxford Agricultural Economics Institute, 1974.

"The Alternatives before Us in Agricultural Development: An Economist's View." In *Proceedings* of the 1974 Wheat, Triticale and Barley Seminar, International Maize and Wheat Improvement Center, El Batan, Mexico, edited by R. G. Anderson, pp. 64–68.

"Conflicts Over Changes in Scarcity: An Economic Approach." *American Journal of Agricultural Economics* 56 (Dec. 1974): 998–1004.

"Investments in Ourselves: Opportunities and Implications." In *The Economics of Education*, edited by Myron H. Ross, pp. 63–70. Ann Arbor, Mich.: University of Michigan, 1974.

"Agriculture in an Unstable Economy—Revisited." *Journal of the Northeastern Agricultural Economics Council* 3 (Oct. 1974): 1–9.

"The Value of the Ability to Deal with Disequilibria." *Journal of Economic Literature* 13, no. 3 (1975): 827–46.

"Food Alternatives Before Us: An Economic Perspective." In *Earth 2020*. Faculty Institute Teachers' Workbook. San Francisco, 1975.

"Knowledge, Agriculture and Welfare." In *Views of Science, Technology and Development*, edited by Eugene and Vivian Rabinowitch, pp. 253–60. Oxford: Pergamon Press, 1975.

"The Politics and Economics of Beef." In *Proceedings* of the Bank of Mexico Conference on Livestock Production in the Tropics, Acapulco, 1976, pp. 63–72.

"The Economic Conditions for Agricultural Modernization." In *Proceedings* of the Bank of Mexico Conference on Livestock Production in the Tropics, Acapulco, 1976, pp. 83–95.

"Uneven Prospects for Gains from Agricultural Research Related to Economic Policy." In *Resource Allocation and Productivity in National and International Agricultural Research*, edited by Thomas M. Arndt, Dana G. Dalrymple, and Vernon Ruttan, pp. 578–89. Minneapolis: University of Minnesota Press, 1977.

"Economics, Farm People and the Political Economy." In *Contemporary Issues in Agricultural and Economic Development of Developing Nations*, pp. 254–68. Nairobi: Nairobi University, East African Literature Bureau, 1977.

"The Hungry, Crowded, Competitive World." *Bulletin of the Atomic Scientist* 33 (Oct. 1977): 254–68.

"Economic Value of Human Time Over Time." In *Lectures in Agricultural Economics*, pp. 1–24. Bicentennial year lectures sponsored by the U.S. Department of Agriculture Economic Research Service. Washington, D.C.: U.S. Department of Agriculture, 1977.

"On Economic History in Extending Economics." *Economic Development and Cultural Change* 25 (1977): 245–53.

"On the Economics of the Increases in the Value of Human Time Over Time." Fifth World Congress of the International Economic Association, Tokyo, 1977. In *Economic Growth and Resources*, vol. 2: *Trends and Factors*, edited by R. C. O. Mathews, pp. 107–29. London: Macmillan, 1980.

"Migration: An Economist's View." In *Human Migration*, edited by William H. McNeil and Ruth Adams, pp. 371–86. Bloomington, Ind.: Indiana University Press, 1978.

"Investment in Population Quality Throughout Low-Income Countries." In *World Population and Development: Challenges and Prospects*, edited by Philip M. Hauser, pp. 339–60. Syracuse, N.Y.: Syracuse University Press, 1979.

"The Economics of Research and Agricultural Productivity." International Agricultural Development Service Occasional Paper. New York, 1979.

"The Value of Higher Education in Low-Income Countries: An Economist's View." In *Higher Education and the New International Order*. Paris: International Institute for Educational Planning, forthcoming.

"Politics Versus Economics in Food and Agriculture Throughout the World." In *Portfolio*, International Economic Perspective, vol. 6, edited by Anne O. Krueger, pp. 1–12. Washington, D.C.: International Communications Agency, 1978.

"Life Span, Health, Savings and Productivity." With Rati Ram. *Economic Development and Cultural Change* 27 (April 1979): 399–421.

"Human Capital Approaches in Organizing and Paying for Education." In *Financing Education: Overcoming Inefficiency and In-equity,* edited by Walter W. McMahon and Terry G. Geske. University of Illinois Press, forthcoming, 1981.

"Investment in Entrepreneurial Ability." *Scandinavian Journal of Economics* 82 (December 1980): n.p.

Congressional Testimony

"Post-War Public Welfare Problems in Agriculture." *National Defense Migration Hearings before the House Committee on Agriculture.* 76th Cong. 1st sess. November 25, 1941, pt. 22.

"Statement on Extension of Reciprocal Trade Agreements Act." *Hearings before the House Committee on Ways and Means.* 78th Cong., 1st sess. April 22, 1943, pp. 715–20.

Hearings before the House Committee on Agriculture. 80th Cong. 1st sess. October 9–10, 1947, pp. 661–82.

"Current Price Developments and the Problem of Economic Stabilization." *Hearings before the Joint Committee on the Economic Report.* 80th Cong. 1st sess. June 1947, pt. 1, pp. 322–35.

"Statement on Foreign Economic Policy." *Hearings before Subcomm. on Foreign Economic Policy of the Joint Committee on the Economic Report.* 84th Cong., 1st sess. November 17, 1955, pp. 577–84.

"A Statement on Agricultural Policy." *Hearings before the Joint Committee on the Economic Report.* 84th Cong., 1st sess. February 2, 1955.

"U.S. Farm Problem in Relation to Growth and Development of U.S. Economy." *Hearings on Policy for Commercial Agriculture before Subcomm. on Agricultural Policy of the Joint Econ. Committee.* 85th Cong., 1st sess. November 22, 1957, pp. 3–14; December 16–20, 1957, pp. 8–9.

"Economic Impact of Science and Technology." *Highlights of Science in the United States: Hearings before Subcomm. of the House Committee on Appropriations.* 87th Cong., 2nd sess. February 27, 1962, pp. 144–54.

"Food for the World: Policy Choices." *World War on Hunger: Hearings before the House Committee on Agriculture.* 89th Cong., 2nd sess. February 14–18, 1966, Serial W, pt. 1, pp. 156–72.

"To Establish a National Institution of Education." *Hearings before Subcomm. of the House Committee on Education.* 92nd Cong., 1st sess. June 14, 1971, pp. 439–44.

Index

Abilities, innate: distribution of, 21
Academic consulting: influence on economic research of, 119, 119n
Actin, Alexander W., 89n
Africa: poverty in, 6
Agency for International Development, U.S. (A.I.D.), 126–27, 133, 136
Agenda (A.I.D. publication), 136
Agriculture: research achievements, 7; disequilibria associated with modernization of, 9–10; incentives distorted by government intervention, 24, 44; role of human capital in, 32; research expenditures in selected low-income countries, 50–51 (table 6); decline in relative contribution of to national income, 60; wage determination in, 63–64; allocation of funds to development of, 129–30; discrimination against, 137
Agriculture, United States Department of (USDA), 113, 134
A.I.D. *See* Agency for International Development, U.S.
Aid: in kind, 131–32; tied, 132. *See also* Foreign aid
Aid agencies, U.S.: personnel costs, 132
Aid capital: malallocation of, 131
Allocation of time: theory of, 61

Allocative ability of nonfarm people, 25
Allocative ability on small-scale producing units, 9
Ames group of economists, 120
Anderson, C. Arnold, 43n, 47
Argentina: education and research impaired by instability, 45; soybean production in, 130
Atkinson, Richard C., 114n

Bangladesh, 135
Barlow, Robin, 38n
Bauer, Peter, 118, 136n
Becker, Gary S., 12n, 30–31, 80n
Behrman, Jere, 38n
Blaug, Mark, 42n
Bombay: incomes contrasted with those in United States, 41
Borkar, G., 38n
Bowman, Mary Jean, 43n, 47, 55n
Boyce, James K., 16n, 50–51n, 107
Brazil: higher-education record of, 45; research viability of, 103; soybean production in, 130
Brookings Institution, 111
Brown, E. H. Phelps, 67, 69 (table 11)
Butz, William P., 30

Canadian International Research Development Centre, 126
Capital: homogeneity assumption,

167

Lightning Source UK Ltd.
Milton Keynes UK
UKHW010105030721
386541UK00001B/28